Table of Contents

The History of the Delicatessen

Delicatessens originated in New York during the middle to late eighteen hundreds and early nineteen hundreds with the influx of Jewish immigrants to the United States from Eastern Europe. Often whole communities emigrated together, in essence taking their entire shtetl (the Yiddish term for a Jewish village or small-town community in the "old country") with them. Poverty was rampant, work was arduous and interminable, and the street was the preferred gathering place for socializing with friends and neighbors. Kosher food that was cheap and could be eaten easily and quickly during inexorable work hours became a necessity. Consequently, "street delis" — peddlers with pushcarts selling pickled cucumbers, herring, bagels, and knishes — became popular and prevalent.

Lone male immigrants, without families to prepare acceptable foods for them, bought additional kosher meals from neighbors. This dearth of kosher alternatives inspired the storefront deli, which commonly enlisted whole families and close friends to make cherished delicacies from the homeland. Some delicatessens were counter-style, providing only prepared foods to go; others were restaurant-style with sit-down service and menus. All were glatt kosher (strictly kosher, according to the Jewish dietary laws of kashruth), which, among other stipulations, forbids the intermingling of meat and dairy products. Therefore, delicatessens served either dairy or meat, never both and never alternating.

The original delis specialized in pickled, cured, and smoked foods that were difficult and time-consuming to prepare at home. As with most ethnic cooking, there were subtle variations in seasonings and techniques, making each deli's offerings distinctive. In addition, specialties varied from deli to deli depending on the family's extraction, country and region of origin, customs, and unique traditions.

The foods were replete with flavor as well as heritage, springing from the wealth of ingenuity and resourcefulness that so often is the legacy of peasant cultures. They were also rich in animal fat, animal protein, and cholesterol, reducing them to less-than-healthful status by modern standards.

Over time, delicatessens became acculturated and lost much of their distinguishing Jewish characteristics. During the mid-nineteen hundreds, when roadside diners became trendy, delicatessens blended further into obscurity by incorporating standard diner fare (such as meat loaf with gravy and macaroni and cheese) among their traditional ethnic selections. Eventually, unheard of combinations that betrayed the deli's kosher beginnings began to emerge. In addition to "kosher-style" options — variations of traditional Jewish dishes that do not adhere to kosher dietary laws — antithetical items, such as Reuben sandwiches containing both meat and cheese, began appearing on delicatessen menus.

Today, virtually all the bona fide kosher delis have disappeared. In their stead are peculiar descendants that belie their roots. The odd deli-diner amalgam that inhabits our present landscape is a distant reminder of a bygone era. Supermarkets, convenience stores, gourmet shops, and natural food markets all have sections designated as "the deli counter." This particular part of the store generally features a cooler full of mayonnaise-saturated salads, fatty cured meats, salt-laden spreads and pickled items, greasy fried foods, rich cheeses, and even pork products and shellfish, which are forbidden by all kosher practices. It seems that the modern interpretation of deli has come to simply connote "prepared foods or foods that require little preparation." These dishes are often far from healthful and frequently are not very ethnic. In contemporary vernacular, "deli" essentially means "fast food."

Reinventing the Past

I have approached this book with the awareness of the rich legacy of the delicatessen, the value of preparing recipes according to the cook's cultural background and individual tastes, and the importance of maintaining the wholesomeness and wholeness of food. With these simple recipes I have tried to preserve the humble traditions of the past while incorporating the healthful trends of the present. This is honest food — pure, natural, and whole. No dairy, no meat, but definitely glatt kosher. Fast food with heart and soul. Deli food made uncommonly good with common, plant-based ingredients.

Some of the recipes presented here do not provide exact measurements. This allows the cook to season the food and adjust amounts to suit varying tastes and appetites. If you like plenty of lemon, by all means use a lot; if you don't care for garlic, leave it out. If something isn't your family's favorite or it's a new dish you're trying out for the first time, prepare less of it. Conversely, if there's something everyone adores, definitely make larger amounts. Use your "cook's intuition," your sixth sense, to judge proper quantities and determine when something is cooked to perfection and adequately seasoned. This will ensure the results are suited to your individual preferences and those for whom you are cooking. Through taste and experience you will soon develop your own deli specialties — foods that reflect your roots and highlight your inventiveness. This is the way our ancestors cooked, regardless of their descent.

Delicious food that brings together people of all origins is the bedrock of families and communities the world over. It is also the ever-present spirit of the delicatessen.

Bringing Home the Deli

Delicatessens typically showcase a wide variety of foods — fresh and marinated salads featuring beans, grains, noodles, vegetables, or fruit; tempting spreads; tangy pickles; hot noodle dishes and casseroles; and soups of every ilk. Vegan Deli is no different, except that all the dishes are made with healthful plant foods.

Select recipes from this book as you would order items from a delicatessen. There are no rules for what goes with what, so you can mix and match to your heart's content. It's fun to prepare several deli items at a time and keep them on hand in the refrigerator. With a variety of deli dishes ready-made, you can create a number of different and exciting meals with very little effort. Here are a few ideas:

- soup + grain salad + bean salad + pickle
- vegetable salad + bean salad + hot grain
- vegetable salad + vegetable salad + bean salad
- potato salad + vegetable salad + pickle
- spread + bread + vegetable salad
- noodle salad + hot vegetable + vegetable salad
- hot casserole + vegetable salad + bean salad
- soup + bread + fruit salad
- soup + potato salad + pickle
- soup + grain salad + vegetable salad

History of the Delicatessen

As you can see, if you have a few different salads already prepared, you can design a meal in a snap. For ease, you could make a couple of salads in an evening or over a weekend. They will keep for several days and can be served throughout the week. Just add a hot grain, soup, vegetable, pickle, or bread, and your dinner can be ready in a flash. Of course, deli food also makes outstanding lunches, brunches, buffet items, and party fare. It is great for share-a-dish gatherings or when company's coming because most dishes can be prepared in advance and served cold or, if necessary, reheated, with no loss of flavor or texture.

It's easy to turn whole foods into fast foods with these simple, timeless recipes. They inspire the imagination and invite creativity. Enter a world of exciting, enticing eating. Welcome to *Vegan Deli!*

Pickled & Marinated Vegetables

Mixed Vegetable Pickle

Makes 1 pound of pickled vegetables

This exciting quick pickle is made with your choice of a multicolored variety of vegetables.

1 pound of mixed vegetables cut into bite-size pieces (or left
    whole, if very small); choose from: cauliflower, carrots,
    fennel, turnips, green beans, bell peppers, baby corn
1 to 2 cloves garlic, sliced
1 bay leaf
2¼ cups water
¼ cup white wine vinegar
1½ tablespoons salt
1½ teaspoons whole black peppercorns
1½ teaspoons whole coriander seeds
Good pinch of cayenne pepper (optional)

1. Pack the vegetables tightly in colorful layers in a 1-quart jar along with the garlic and bay leaf. Place the water, vinegar, salt, peppercorns, coriander seeds, and cayenne pepper, if using, in a small saucepan, and bring to a boil. Simmer 3 to 4 minutes, then pour immediately over the vegetables in the jar. It should cover the vegetables completely. Cool.

2. Put the lid on the jar, and store in the refrigerator. The pickle will be ready to eat in 3 to 4 days, but will keep for several weeks.

Per ¼ cup: Calories 8, Protein 0 g, Carbohydrates 2 g, Fat 0 g

Pickled & Marinated Vegetables

Vinegared Mixed Vegetables

Makes 8 servings

This colorful pickle is quick and delicious. It makes an excellent alternative to crudités for a party or, if the pieces are very small, a lovely relish.

½ head of cauliflower, cut into small florets
2 carrots, cut into matchsticks or thinly sliced
2 zucchini, cut into matchsticks or thinly sliced
2 stalks celery, thinly sliced
Lots of salt
½ cup wine vinegar
2 to 3 teaspoons extra-virgin olive oil (optional)

1. Combine all the vegetables in a large bowl. Sprinkle very liberally with salt, stir, and let rest for 1 hour.

2. Stir in the vinegar, mix well, and let rest for another hour. Drain well in a colander. (The salt will drain off with the vegetable juices and vinegar.)

3. Dress with the olive oil just before serving, if desired.

Per serving: Calories 22, Protein 1 g, Carbohydrates 5 g, Fat 0 g

Salt Pickles

Makes as much as you like.

Mixed vegetables: cauliflower cut into florets, sliced carrots,
    thin green beans, small asparagus, sugar snap peas
Salt
Fresh lemon juice
Extra-virgin olive oil

1. Layer the vegetables in a colander, sprinkling each layer
liberally with salt. Let sit for 3 to 4 hours to draw out the
juices.

2. Rinse, drain, and pat dry. Dress with a mixture of lemon
juice and olive oil. Let marinate for several hours or several
days in the refrigerator. These pickles will keep for about a
week.

Pickled & Marinated Vegetables

Hot and Spicy Pickled Cabbage

Makes 4 to 6 servings

Galvanize your taste buds with this garlicky hot and sour pickle.

2 cups very thinly sliced or shredded white or green cabbage
¼ cup fresh lemon juice
½ teaspoon salt
¼ to ½ teaspoon crushed garlic
¼ teaspoon hot red pepper flakes or a good pinch of cayenne
    pepper

Place all the ingredients in a large bowl, and toss together to
mix well. Chill for at least 1 hour before serving.

Per serving: Calories 10, Protein 0 g, Carbohydrates 2 g, Fat 0 g

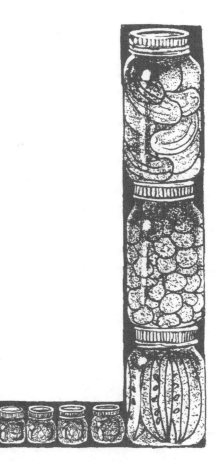

Pickled & Marinated Vegetables

Garlic Dill Pickles

Makes 1 pound of pickles

Making homemade dill pickles is somewhat of an art. It's not at all difficult, and after a while you develop a taste for which seasonings to include and how much salt to use.

1 pound kirby cucumbers or other small cucumbers
3 sprigs fresh dill
3 whole cloves garlic, peeled and sliced in half lengthwise
½ teaspoon whole black peppercorns

Flavoring Options:
1 to 2 bay leaves
½ teaspoon whole yellow mustard seeds
4 whole cloves
Tiny piece of fresh gingerroot

3 cups water
1½ tablespoons salt
2 teaspoons white wine vinegar
1½ teaspoons sugar (optional)

Pickled & Marinated Vegetables

1. Scrub the cucumbers well and pack them into a 1-quart jar along with the dill, garlic, peppercorns, and any additional flavoring options that you choose.

2. Combine the water, salt, vinegar, and sugar (if using) in a saucepan, and bring to a boil. Pour immediately over the cucumbers; the liquid should cover them completely. Cool. Then put the lid on the jar, and store in the refrigerator. The pickles will be ready to eat in 4 to 6 days, but will keep for several weeks.

Per 2 oz. serving: Calories 8, Protein 0 g, Carbohydrates 2 g, Fat 0 g

Tip:
• The pickles will be "half sour" in 4 to 5 days, "fully sour" in 6 to 8. The longer they marinate, the more sour they will become.

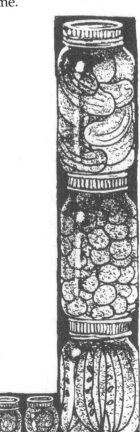

Pickled & Marinated Vegetables

Pickled Beets

Makes 6 to 8 servings

In this timeless recipe, beets are marinated in tantalizing, aromatic spices. It's an enticing treatment that is irresistible.

10 to 12 fresh small baby beets (or 6 to 8 medium beets)
1 cup red wine vinegar
1 cup water
¼ cup sugar
1 teaspoon salt
10 whole allspice berries
6 whole cloves
3 bay leaves
½ stick of cinnamon

1. Trim the beets leaving an inch or two of the stem end intact; do not trim the root. Scrub well and place in a large saucepan or Dutch oven. Cover with water and bring to a boil. Moderate the heat, cover, and simmer until fork tender, about 30 to 40 minutes depending on the size of the beets. Uncover and cool in the cooking liquid; then drain well and peel. The stem end and skin will slip off just using your hands. Slice off the root tail with a knife.

Pickled & Marinated Vegetables

2. If using small beets, keep whole. If using medium size beets, halve or quarter them. Pack into a 1-quart jar.

3. Place the vinegar, water, sugar, salt, allspice, cloves, bay leaves, and cinnamon stick in a saucepan, and bring to a boil. Moderate the heat and simmer for 5 minutes. Pour immediately over the beets. The liquid should cover the beets completely. Cool.

4. Put the lid on the jar, and store in the refrigerator. The beets will be ready to eat in 24 hours but will keep for several weeks.

Per serving: Calories 52, Protein 1 g, Carbohydrates 12 g, Fat 0 g

Tip:
• If you are lucky enough to find fresh beets with the greens intact, be sure to save them. Cook the greens like kale or chard. They make a flavorful and nutritious vegetable dish.

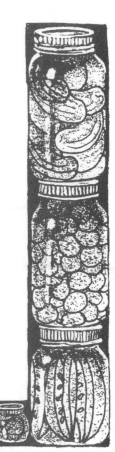

Pickled & Marinated Vegetables

Polish Sweet and Sour Zucchini Pickles

Makes about 1 pound of pickles

Polish Jews are famous for their sweet and sour dishes. This simple pickle is representative of those tantalizing flavors.

3 small zucchinis, sliced into ¼-inch rounds
1 white onion, cut in half and thinly sliced
1 cup apple cider vinegar
2 tablespoons sugar
¼ teaspoon whole yellow mustard seeds
¼ teaspoon whole celery seeds
¼ teaspoon ground turmeric

1. Layer the sliced zucchini and onion in a 1-quart jar. Combine the vinegar, sugar, mustard seeds, celery seeds, and turmeric in a saucepan, and bring to a boil. Pour immediately over the zucchini and onions; the liquid should cover them completely. Cool.

2. Put the lid on the jar, and store in the refrigerator. The pickles will be ready to eat in 24 to 48 hours, but will keep for several weeks.

Per 2 oz. serving: Calories 35, Protein 1 g, Carbohydrates 8 g, Fat 0 g

Pickled & Marinated Vegetables

Pickled Eggplant "Herring"

Makes 4 to 6 servings

This dish tastes so amazingly like the "real thing" you'll think there's something fishy.

1 medium eggplant, peeled
1 small mild onion, cut in half and thinly sliced
1 cup white wine vinegar (or apple cider vinegar)
2 tablespoons sugar
6 whole peppercorns
6 whole cloves
1 whole bay leaf

1. Cut the eggplant into equal-size chunks, and place in a bowl. Sprinkle liberally all over with salt, and let rest for 1 hour. Transfer to a colander. Rinse well and pat dry.

2. Place the onion in a separate small bowl, and sprinkle liberally all over with salt. Let rest for 1 hour while the eggplant rests. Transfer to a colander or large wire mesh strainer, and rinse well.

3. Steam the eggplant until just tender but still very firm, about 8 minutes depending on the size of the chunks. Layer with the onion in a glass or ceramic bowl or casserole.

4. Combine the vinegar, sugar, peppercorns, cloves, and bay leaf in a saucepan. Bring to a boil and simmer 5 minutes. Pour over the eggplant and onion. Cool. Cover tightly and chill in the refrigerator several hours or overnight.

Per serving: Calories 68, Protein 1 g, Carbohydrates 17 g, Fat 0 g

Variation:
• After the eggplant has marinated, drain off the liquid and stir in 1 cup Sour Dressing, p. 123.

Pickled & Marinated Vegetables

Russian-Style Chopped Eggplant "Herring"

Makes 6 servings

Healthful herring? This recipe proves that it's not only possible, it's delicious!

1 medium eggplant, peeled
Salt
1 small mild onion, finely minced
2 thin slices whole grain bread (crusts removed), finely
    crumbed between your fingers
2 tablespoons wine vinegar (or apple cider vinegar or fresh
    lemon juice)
1 tablespoon extra-virgin olive oil
2 teaspoons sugar

1. Cut the eggplant into equal-size chunks, and place in a bowl. Sprinkle liberally all over with salt, and let sit for 1 hour. Transfer to a colander. Rinse well and pat dry.

2. Place the onion in a separate small bowl, and sprinkle liberally all over with salt. Let sit for 1 hour while the eggplant sits. Transfer to a wire mesh strainer, and rinse well.

3. Steam the eggplant until just tender but still very firm, about 8 minutes depending on the size of the chunks. Mince very finely. Transfer to a bowl with the onion and crumbed bread. Stir in the vinegar, oil, and sugar, and mix well. Refrigerate several hours before serving.

Per serving: Calories 73, Protein 1 g, Carbohydrates 11 g, Fat 2 g

Variation:
• Add ½ cup Sour Dressing, p. 123.

Pickled & Marinated Vegetables

Marinated Mushrooms

Makes 4 to 6 servings

Simple but deeply flavored.

8 ounces fresh small, whole button mushrooms (If only large
    mushrooms are available, cut them in half or quarters.)
1/2 cup wine vinegar
1 1/2 tablespoons extra-virgin olive oil
1 teaspoon sugar
1 teaspoon Dijon mustard
1/2 teaspoon crushed garlic
1/2 teaspoon dried oregano
1/4 teaspoon dried basil
Salt

1. Clean the mushrooms and pat dry. Place in a bowl and set
aside.

2. Whisk together the remaining ingredients in a small
saucepan, and bring to a boil. Remove from the heat and
pour immediately over the mushrooms. Toss to mix thoroughly. Cool, cover tightly, and chill several hours or
overnight, tossing occasionally.

3. Drain before serving or serve using a slotted spoon.

Per serving: Calories 38, Protein 1 g, Carbohydrates 4 g, Fat 2 g

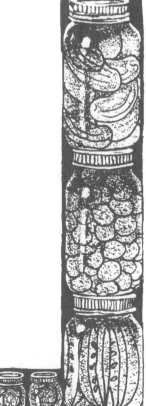

Pickled & Marinated Vegetables

Marinated Carrot Sticks

Makes 6 to 8 servings

Serve marinated carrot sticks as a special appetizer, side dish, or tasty addition to a vegetarian antipasto. They are also great to keep in the fridge for a quick, no-fuss, no-muss snack.

8 to 10 carrots, cut into sticks approximately 2½ inches long x
    ½ inch thick
⅓ cup wine vinegar
¼ cup extra-virgin olive oil
½ teaspoon crushed garlic
Generous pinch of salt
Minced flat-leaf parsley for garnish (optional)

1. Place an inch of water in a large saucepan, and bring to a boil. Add the carrots, cover, and cook over medium heat until tender-crisp, about 6 to 8 minutes. Drain and transfer to a bowl.

2. Combine the remaining ingredients in a small bowl or measuring cup, and whisk them together until blended. Pour over the carrots and toss until evenly coated. Cover tightly and refrigerate several hours or overnight, tossing again once or twice. Bring to room temperature before serving. Drain or serve with a slotted spoon. Garnish with parsley, if desired.

Per serving: Calories 58, Protein 1 g, Carbohydrates 9 g, Fat 1 g

Vegetable Salads

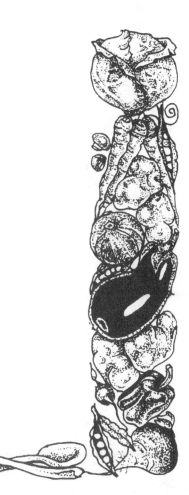

Diced Raw Vegetable Salad

Makes 8 servings

A simple and versatile salad that is a snap to prepare.

1 head Romaine lettuce or 2 heads bibb lettuce
2 ripe tomatoes
1 cucumber, peeled
1 green bell pepper (optional)
8 red radishes (optional)
Minced mild red onions or thinly sliced scallions
Minced fresh parsley or dill
3 to 4 tablespoons fresh lemon juice
3 tablespoons extra-virgin olive oil
Salt and pepper

Finely chop or dice the lettuce, tomatoes, cucumber, pepper, and radishes, if using. Place in a bowl along with the onion and parsley or dill. Dress with the lemon juice, oil, salt, and pepper just before serving.

Per serving: Calories 62, Protein 0 g, Carbohydrates 3 g, Fat 5 g

Tunisian Boiled Vegetable Salad

Makes 8 to 10 servings

Flavorful spices transform modest vegetables into an exotic delicacy.

4 carrots, trimmed and scraped
3 celery stalks
3 waxy potatoes
1 small cauliflower
¼ cup extra-virgin olive oil
¼ cup fresh lemon juice
1½ teaspoons paprika
1½ teaspoons ground caraway
1 teaspoon ground coriander
¼ teaspoon cayenne pepper
Salt

1. Cut the vegetables into ¾-inch pieces. Bring a large pot of salted water to a boil. Add the carrots and celery, and simmer for 5 minutes. Add the potatoes and continue to simmer for 5 minutes. Add the cauliflower and simmer 5 to 10 minutes longer, or until all the vegetables are tender. Drain well.

2. In a large bowl, whisk together the remaining ingredients. Add the drained vegetables and mix well. Serve warm or thoroughly chilled.

Per serving: Calories 127, Protein 1 g, Carbohydrates 17 g, Fat 6 g

Vegetable Salads

Red and White Cabbage Salad

Makes 4 to 6 servings

Eye catching, easy, quick, and delicious.

2 cups shredded red cabbage
2 cups shredded white or green cabbage
¼ cup fresh lemon juice
2 tablespoons extra-virgin olive oil
Salt

Place the all ingredients in a large bowl, and toss together to mix well. Chill in the refrigerator for at least 1 hour before serving.

Per serving: Calories 65, Protein 0 g, Carbohydrates 4 g, Fat 6 g

Tang Tsel

Makes 4 servings

Although this simple mixed vegetable salad is not standard deli fare, it is very, very good.

1 cup thinly sliced or shredded green cabbage
1 cup thinly sliced or shredded red cabbage
1 small tomato, seeded and sliced into thin slivers
¼ cup brown rice vinegar
1 tablespoon toasted sesame oil

Combine the cabbage and tomato in a medium bowl, and toss together. Sprinkle vinegar and sesame oil over the vegetables, and toss again to mix thoroughly. Serve at once or chill.

Per serving: Calories 49, Protein 0 g, Carbohydrates 4 g, Fat 2 g

Vegetable Salads

Vinaigrette Coleslaw

Makes 4 servings

A delectable slaw with a few special flourishes.

3 cups finely chopped or shredded green cabbage
1 large carrot, shredded
1 green bell pepper, minced (optional)
3 tablespoons grated mild onion
3 tablespoons extra-virgin olive oil
2 tablespoons white wine vinegar
1 teaspoon sugar
½ teaspoon prepared yellow mustard
Salt and white pepper

1. Combine the cabbage, carrot, pepper, if using, and onion in a large bowl, and toss together.

2. Whisk together the remaining ingredients, and pour over the vegetables. Mix thoroughly. Chill for at least 1 hour before serving.

Per serving: Calories 117, Protein 1 g, Carbohydrates 6 g, Fat 9 g

Variation:
• For **Creamy Coleslaw**, use ½ cup Deli Dressing, p. 122, or vegan mayonnaise in place of the oil.

Vegetable Salads

Caper and Dill Coleslaw

Makes 4 to 6 servings

Capers and dill add a refreshing twist to this popular deli staple.

3 cups finely chopped or shredded green cabbage
1 cup finely chopped or shredded red cabbage
2 medium carrots, shredded
½ cup Deli Dressing, p. 122, or vegan mayonnaise
2 teaspoons capers, drained
2 teaspoons dried dill
¼ teaspoon crushed garlic

1. Combine the cabbage and carrot in a large bowl, and toss together.

2. Whirl the remaining ingredients in a blender or food processor until smooth and creamy. Pour over the cabbage and carrots, and toss to thoroughly combine.

Per serving: Calories 82, Protein 1 g, Carbohydrates 7 g, Fat 5 g

Vegetable Salads

Cabbage Salad
with Cumin or Caraway

Makes 4 to 6 servings

A little spice adds enormous flavor and flair.

4 cups finely shredded green cabbage
3 tablespoons extra-virgin olive oil
1 teaspoon ground cumin or caraway
Salt and cayenne pepper

Combine all the ingredients in a large bowl, and toss thoroughly.

Per serving: Calories 84, Protein 0 g, Carbohydrates 3 g, Fat 8 g

Apple and Nut Slaw

Makes 6 servings

A little bit sweet, a little bit crunchy, this healthful salad is one even children can't resist.

4 cups shredded green cabbage
2 crisp red apples, diced
1 cup coarsely chopped walnuts
½ cup raisins (optional)
Approx. ½ cup Deli Dressing, p. 122, or vegan mayonnaise

Combine the cabbage, apples, walnuts, and raisins, if using, in a large bowl. Add enough dressing to moisten, and toss thoroughly.

Per serving: Calories 213, Protein 3 g, Carbohydrates 14 g, Fat 15 g

Vegetable Salads

Radish Salad

Makes 4 servings

This traditional Russian salad is usually made with large, strong-tasting black radishes, but other radishes will work just fine.

12 ounces radishes, trimmed and grated or thinly sliced
3 tablespoons extra-virgin olive oil
Grated onion
Salt and pepper

Combine the radishes and olive oil in a bowl. Season with grated onion, salt, and pepper, and toss well.

Per serving: Calories 105, Protein 0 g, Carbohydrates 3 g, Fat 9 g

Variation:
• For **Creamed Radish Salad**, omit the olive oil and onion, and dress with 1¼ cups Sour Dressing, p. 123.

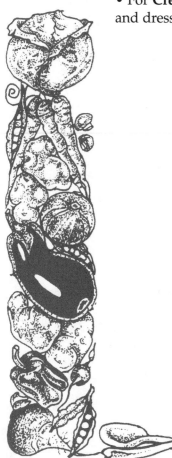

Vegetable Salads

Spicy Cucumber Salad

Makes 4 servings

This refreshing salad is aromatic and tantalizing with just a bit of a pungent bite.

2 cups thinly sliced English cucumbers
Salt
2 tablespoons brown rice vinegar
1 tablespoon toasted sesame oil
Pinch of cayenne pepper

1. Sprinkle the cucumbers with plenty of salt, and leave to drain in a colander for at least 30 minutes until they soften and lose their juices. Rinse under cold water and drain well.

2. Transfer to a medium bowl, and sprinkle with the vinegar and oil. Season with cayenne pepper, and toss to mix thoroughly. Serve at once or chill.

Per serving: Calories 51, Protein 1 g, Carbohydrates 4 g, Fat 3 g

Vegetable Salads

Vinegared Cucumbers

Makes 4 servings

This salad is light and refreshing, with a delicate Polish-style sweet-and-sour flavor.

2 cups thinly sliced English cucumbers
Salt
2 tablespoons vinegar of your choice
1 teaspoon sugar
Grated onion (optional)
Pepper

1. Sprinkle the cucumbers with plenty of salt, and leave to drain in a colander for at least 30 minutes until they soften and lose their juices. Rinse under cold water and drain well.

2. Combine the vinegar and sugar in a medium bowl. Add the cucumber and a little grated onion, if desired. Mix well. Season with salt and pepper, and mix again.

Per serving: Calories 47, Protein 2 g, Carbohydrates 6 g, Fat 2 g

Vegetable Salads

Cucumber Salad
with Sour Dressing

Makes 4 servings

A light, creamy salad that is the perfect companion for vinaigrette salads and dry-textured hot dishes.

2 cups thinly sliced English cucumbers
Salt
¼ cup Sour Dressing, p. 123
2 tablespoons vinegar (your choice)
1 teaspoon sugar

1. Sprinkle the cucumbers with plenty of salt, and leave to drain in a colander for at least 30 minutes until they soften and lose their juices. Rinse under cold water and drain well.

2. Combine the Sour Dressing, vinegar, and sugar in a medium bowl. Add the cucumbers and mix well.

Per serving: Calories 46, Protein 2 g, Carbohydrates 6 g, Fat 2 g

Vegetable Salads

Creamed Cucumbers
with Walnuts and Dill

Makes 4 servings

This is a fabulous and unusual way to serve cucumbers — very refreshing and flavorful. Don't keep it for more than a day or so though, because after a while the acid in the dressing causes the walnuts to give the salad a purplish tint. It will still be highly delicious and edible, just a little less appetizing to look at.

2 cups English cucumbers, cut into ¼-inch cubes
¾ teaspoon dried dill
1½ cups Sour Dressing, p. 123
¼ cup finely chopped walnuts

Place the cucumbers in a medium bowl. Stir the dill into the dressing, and pour over the cucumbers. Add the walnuts and toss to mix thoroughly. Chill for an hour before serving.

Per serving: Calories 198, Protein 9 g, Carbohydrates 9 g, Fat 14 g

Vegetable Salads

Creamed Cucumbers and Onion with Mint

Makes 4 servings

Onion and mint add a vibrant, fresh flavor to this unpretentious dish.

2 cups thinly sliced English cucumbers
½ small mild onion, very thinly sliced
Salt
1½ cups Sour Dressing, p. 123
1½ tablespoons chopped fresh mint, or 1½ teaspoons dried
    spearmint

1. Sprinkle the cucumbers and onion with plenty of salt, and leave to drain in a colander for at least 30 minutes until they soften and lose their juices. Rinse under cold water and drain well. Transfer to a medium bowl.

2. Stir the mint into the Sour Dressing. Pour over the cucumbers and onion, and toss to mix thoroughly. Serve at once or chilled.

Per serving: Calories 156, Protein 8 g, Carbohydrates 9 g, Fat 10 g

Vegetable Salads

Green Bean and Tomato Salad

Makes 4 servings

Use tender young beans, as they will make the most delectable salad.

2 cups fresh green beans, trimmed and cut into 2-inch pieces
1 medium tomato
1 tablespoon red wine vinegar
1 tablespoon extra-virgin olive oil
1 teaspoon natural soy sauce

1. Steam the green beans until just tender, about 10 minutes. Place in a large bowl.

2. Cut the tomato into 12 thin wedges, and add to the green beans.

3. Combine the vinegar, oil, and soy sauce in a small measuring cup or bowl, and beat together with a fork or mini-whisk until well combined. Pour over the vegetables and toss gently. Let marinate at room temperature for 30 to 60 minutes before serving. Store leftovers in the refrigerator but bring to room temperature about 30 minutes before serving.

Per serving: Calories 54, Protein 1 g, Carbohydrates 5 g, Fat 2 g

Vegetable Salads

Roasted Green Peppers with Tomatoes

Makes 4 to 6 servings

Roasted bell peppers lend a smoky essence to this unique salad.

3 large green bell peppers
3 large tomatoes, cut into 6 wedges per tomato
3 tablespoons fresh lemon juice
2 tablespoons extra-virgin olive oil
Salt

1. Heat the broiler. Place the whole peppers on a dry baking sheet, then place the baking sheet under the broiler a few inches from the heat source. Roast, turning once or twice, until softened and the skin is charred and blistered.

2. Remove from the oven and place in a pot with a tight fitting lid. Allow the peppers to steam for about 15 minutes to loosen the skins. When cool enough to handle, peel off the loosened skin with your fingers and remove the stems, seeds, and ribs. Do not rinse the peppers under water as this will wash away the flavor.

3. Cut the peppers into wide strips, then arrange with the tomatoes on a serving platter. Whisk together the lemon juice, oil, and salt, and pour over the vegetables. Serve at room temperature.

Per serving: Calories 75, Protein 1 g, Carbohydrates 6 g, Fat 6 g

Vegetable Salads

Red Pepper Lox

Makes 4 servings

Red Pepper Lox is a delicacy dressed simply with olive oil and a pinch of salt. Perfect for bagels, of course. Try them atop your favorite nondairy cream cheese. You can heighten the flavor further, if you like, with a little vinegar, garlic, and cayenne.

2 large red bell peppers
2 tablespoons extra-virgin olive oil
2 tablespoons wine vinegar or fresh lemon juice (optional)
Crushed garlic (optional)
Cayenne pepper (optional)
Salt

1. Heat the broiler. Place the whole peppers on a dry baking sheet, then place the baking sheet under the broiler a few inches from the heat source. Roast, turning once or twice, until softened and the skin is charred and blistered.

2. Remove from the oven and place in a pot with a tight fitting lid. Allow the peppers to steam for about 15 minutes to loosen the skins. When cool enough to handle, peel off the loosened skin with your fingers and remove the stems, seeds, and ribs. Do not rinse the peppers under water as this will wash away the flavor.

Vegetable Salads

3. Cut into wide strips. Dress as desired with olive oil, vinegar, garlic, cayenne, and salt. Cover tightly and let marinate several hours or overnight in the refrigerator. Remove from the marinade to serve.

Per serving: Calories 40, Protein 0 g, Carbohydrates 2 g, Fat 3 g

Tips:
• Choose heavy peppers with a thick, meaty flesh. Light, thin peppers will burn before their skin chars.

• Jarred roasted red bell peppers are available in most supermarkets and may be substituted for the home-roasted peppers, if preferred.

Vegetable Salads

Fried Pepper and Tomato Salad

Makes 8 servings

This unusual dish is more like a vegetable jam or spread than a conventional salad. It is traditionally served on bread accompanied with fresh lemon wedges.

4 red bell peppers, cut into ¾-inch pieces
2 tablespoons extra-virgin olive oil
2 ripe tomatoes, chopped
½ teaspoon crushed garlic
1 to 2 teaspoons sugar
Salt and pepper

Heat the oil in a large skillet. Add the peppers and fry over low heat until soft and lightly browned. Add the tomatoes, garlic, sugar, salt, and pepper, and simmer, uncovered, until the mixture is very thick, about 30 minutes. Serve warm or cold.

Per serving: Calories 48, Protein 0 g, Carbohydrates 4 g, Fat 2 g

Vegetable Salads

Red Pepper Relish

Makes 4 servings

This delightful relish makes an excellent condiment for sandwiches or an intriguing side dish or salad with meals.

3 red bell peppers
½ teaspoon crushed garlic
3 tablespoons fresh lemon juice
1 tablespoon extra-virgin olive oil
1 teaspoon ground coriander
Salt and cayenne pepper

1. Mince the peppers as finely as possible. Mash them together with the garlic either by hand or in a food processor.

2. Transfer to a bowl and add the remaining ingredients. Mix well. Serve thoroughly chilled.

Per serving: Calories 46, Protein 0 g, Carbohydrates 3 g, Fat 2 g

Vegetable Salads

Cooked Red Pepper Salad

Makes 4 servings

Simple and simply ravishing!

1 tablespoon extra-virgin olive oil
3 red bell peppers, finely minced
¼ cup fresh lemon juice
1 teaspoon ground coriander
½ teaspoon crushed garlic
Salt and cayenne pepper
Minced fresh parsley

Heat the oil in a large skillet. Add the minced peppers, lemon juice, coriander, garlic, salt, and cayenne. Simmer uncovered until the peppers are tender. Chill thoroughly. Garnish with the parsley just before serving.

Per serving: Calories 47, Protein 0 g, Carbohydrates 4 g, Fat 2 g

Vegetable Salads

Pilaki
(Cooked Vegetable Salad)

Makes 6 to 8 servings

A salad of chilled cooked vegetables infused with a light but captivating dressing.

3 tablespoons extra-virgin olive oil
2 large onions, cut in half and sliced
½ teaspoon crushed garlic
4 green bell peppers, sliced into narrow strips
2 large tomatoes, chopped
1 teaspoon ground cumin
Good pinch of cayenne pepper
¾ cup water
Salt and pepper
3 tablespoons fresh lemon juice
Minced fresh parsley (optional)

1. Heat the oil in a large skillet. Add the onions and garlic, and sauté until the onions are soft. Add the green peppers, tomatoes, cumin, and cayenne, and sauté for 5 minutes.

2. Add the water and bring to a simmer. Simmer, uncovered, stirring occasionally, until the liquid has cooked off and the peppers are tender, about 40 to 45 minutes.

3. Season with the lemon juice, salt, and pepper, and chill thoroughly. Garnish with parsley just before serving, if desired.

Per serving: Calories 85, Protein 1 g, Carbohydrates 7 g, Fat 6 g

Vegetable Salads

Beet and Olive Salad

Makes 4 servings

Densely colored beets add a touch of regal elegance to any meal.

2 cups cooked beets, peeled, cut in half, and thinly sliced
2 thin slices mild onion, cut into julienne strips
¼ cup pitted olives of your choice
2 tablespoons wine vinegar
1 tablespoon extra-virgin olive oil
1 teaspoon sugar
¼ teaspoon crushed garlic

Put the beets, onion, and olives in a large bowl. Whisk together the vinegar, olive oil, sugar, and garlic. Pour over the vegetables and toss to coat evenly. Serve at room temperature or thoroughly chilled.

Per serving: Calories 69, Protein 1 g, Carbohydrates 6 g, Fat 5 g

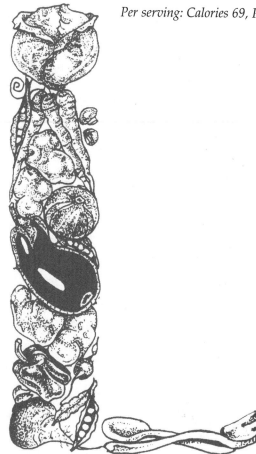

Vegetable Salads

Beet Salad in Sour Dressing

Makes 4 to 6 servings

Even people who turn their noses up at beets find this salad irresistible.

6 cooked and peeled beets, diced (about 5 cups)
2 to 4 tablespoons minced mild onion (optional)
2 tablespoons vinegar or fresh lemon juice
1 tablespoon sugar
Salt
⅓ cup Sour Dressing, p. 123

Combine the beets and onion in a bowl. Dress with the vinegar or lemon juice, sugar, and salt. Stir in the Sour Dressing and mix well. Serve at once or chill.

Per serving: Calories 52, Protein 2 g, Carbohydrates 7 g, Fat 2 g

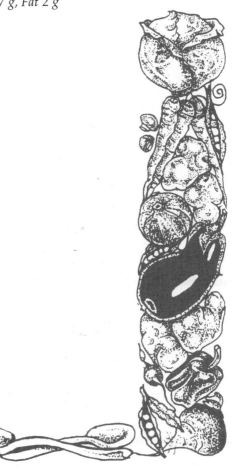

Vegetable Salads

Spiced Beet Salad

Makes 6 servings

Sweet and savory spices blend with the natural sweetness of beets to create a delicate and enchanting taste.

6 cooked beets, peeled and diced (about 5 cups)
3 tablespoons fresh lemon juice
2 tablespoons extra-virgin olive oil
½ teaspoon ground cumin
½ teaspoon paprika
¼ teaspoon cinnamon
Salt and pepper
2 tablespoons minced fresh parsley

Toss the beets with all the ingredients except the parsley. Chill thoroughly. Toss with the parsley just before serving.

Per serving: Calories 57, Protein 0 g, Carbohydrates 4 g, Fat 4 g

Simple Wilted Spinach Salad

Makes 4 servings

A quick, warm salad with a fresh taste and brilliant green color.

1 pound spinach leaves, stems removed
Salt
2 tablespoons extra-virgin olive oil
1 tablespoon fresh lemon juice

Wash the spinach, drain, and squeeze out the excess water with your hands. Put in a large skillet with a pinch of salt, cover, and steam until the leaves collapse. Drain well. Dress with the oil and lemon juice.

Per serving: Calories 85, Protein 2 g, Carbohydrates 3 g, Fat 7 g

Vegetable Salads

Broccoli and Walnut Salad

Makes 6 servings

Crunchy nuts and colorful, sweet-tart fruit turn ordinary broccoli into an extraordinary treat.

6 cups broccoli florets
2 tablespoons extra-virgin olive oil
1 tablespoon vinegar
¼ teaspoon crushed garlic
Cayenne pepper
⅓ cup chopped walnuts
A few tablespoons of pomegranate seeds or finely diced dried
    apricots

1. Steam the broccoli until tender-crisp. Transfer to a bowl.

2. Whisk together the oil, vinegar, garlic, and cayenne, and drizzle over the broccoli. Toss gently. Arrange on a large, flat platter, and sprinkle with the walnuts and fruit.

Per serving: Calories 104, Protein 2 g, Carbohydrates 5 g, Fat 8 g

Vegetable Salads

Sesame Broccoli

Makes 6 servings

Plain broccoli gets all dressed up in this sensational salad.

6 cups broccoli florets
2 tablespoons extra-virgin olive oil
1 red bell pepper, sliced into matchsticks
½ teaspoon crushed garlic
2 tablespoons lightly toasted sesame seeds
1 tablespoon dark sesame oil
Salt or natural soy sauce

1. Steam the broccoli until tender-crisp. Transfer to a bowl.

2. Heat the olive oil in a skillet. Add the red bell pepper, and sauté until tender. Stir in the garlic and cook for 30 seconds. Remove from the heat and pour over the broccoli. Add the remaining ingredients and toss gently. Serve warm or thoroughly chilled.

Per serving: Calories 105, Protein 2 g, Carbohydrates 5 g, Fat 8 g

Vegetable Salads

Copper Penny Salad

Makes 6 servings

Perfect for picnics, parties, or family-style meals, this sweet-and-sour salad appeals to all ages.

1½ pounds carrots
¼ cup extra-virgin olive oil
1 small onion, finely chopped
1 small green bell pepper, finely chopped
One 6-ounce can unsalted tomato paste
½ cup water
¼ cup fresh lemon juice
¼ cup brown sugar
Salt

1. Slice the carrots into ¼-inch circles. Steam until tender and transfer to a bowl.

2. Meanwhile, heat the oil in a large skillet or saucepan. Add the onion and green pepper, and sauté until very tender and starting to brown. Add the remaining ingredients and simmer for 5 minutes. Pour over the carrots and mix gently. Chill thoroughly before serving.

Per serving: Calories 187, Protein 2 g, Carbohydrates 24 g, Fat 9 g

Vegetable Salads

Grated Carrot Salad

Makes 4 to 6 servings

This simple carrot salad is light, fresh, and brimming with wondrous flavor.

1 pound carrots, grated
¼ cup fresh lemon juice
3 tablespoons extra-virgin olive oil
Salt and pepper
¼ cup minced fresh cilantro or parsley

Place the grated carrots in a bowl. Dress with the lemon juice, oil, salt, and pepper. Stir in the cilantro or parsley.

Per serving: Calories 115, Protein 1 g, Carbohydrates 10 g, Fat 8 g

Carrot and Raisin Salad

Makes 4 to 6 servings

The striking combination of unexpected flavors turns commonplace ingredients into a masterpiece.

1 pound carrots, grated
¼ cup raisins
¼ cup orange juice
3 tablespoons extra-virgin olive oil
¼ teaspoon crushed garlic
Pinch of salt

Place the grated carrots and raisins in a bowl. Whisk together the orange juice, oil, garlic, and salt. Pour over the carrots and raisins, and toss well.

Per serving: Calories 138, Protein 1 g, Carbohydrates 15 g, Fat 8 g

Vegetable Salads

Carrot Salad
with Caraway Seeds

Makes 6 servings

Tender-crisp disks of colorful carrots are bathed in a gently spiced dressing and chilled to utter perfection.

1½ pounds carrots, sliced
¼ cup fresh lemon juice
3 tablespoons extra-virgin olive oil
½ teaspoon crushed garlic
1 teaspoon whole or ground caraway seeds
Salt and pepper

Steam the carrots until tender. Alternatively, boil in lightly salted water until tender and drain. Transfer to a bowl and dress with the remaining ingredients. Chill thoroughly before serving.

Per serving: Calories 111, Protein 1 g, Carbohydrates 12 g, Fat 7 g

Variation:
• For **Carrot Salad with Cumin**, replace the caraway seeds with 1 teaspoon ground cumin and a good pinch of paprika.

Vegetable Salads

Braised Celery Salad

Makes 6 servings

Plebian celery rises to royal heights with this unusual but tasty treatment.

1 pound celery, sliced
¼ cup extra-virgin olive oil
¼ cup fresh lemon juice
1 tablespoon sugar
Salt

Combine all the ingredients in a large pan, and bring to a boil. Reduce the heat to low, cover, and simmer for 30 to 45 minutes, or until the celery is very soft and tender. Serve warm or thoroughly chilled.

Per serving: Calories 101, Protein 0 g, Carbohydrates 5 g, Fat 9 g

Vegetable Salads

Roasted Onion Salad

Makes 8 to 10 servings

Soft-cooked onions are lightly dressed and chilled to create an elegant, gourmet delight.

5 medium onions
¼ cup extra-virgin olive oil
2 tablespoons wine vinegar or fresh lemon juice
Salt
Capers, rinsed and squeezed (optional)

1. Preheat the oven to 350°F. Place the whole onions on a baking sheet lined with foil. Bake until tender and soft when pressed, about 1 to 1½ hours. Cool. Peel off and discard the outer skin, cut the onions into quarters, and transfer to a bowl.

2. Dress with the oil, vinegar or lemon juice, and salt. Stir in the capers, if using. Chill thoroughly before serving.

Per serving: Calories 83, Protein 1 g, Carbohydrates 7 g, Fat 6 g

Vegetable Salads

Eggplant Caviar

Makes about 2 cups

Nothing impresses like "caviar." Serve this vegetable delicacy with crackers or toast points or as a small side salad on a bed of tender butterhead lettuce.

1 pound eggplants
2 small tomatoes, finely diced
2 tablespoons finely minced mild onion
2 to 3 tablespoons fresh lemon juice
2 tablespoons extra-virgin olive oil
Salt

1. Prick the eggplants all over with a fork. Place on a dry baking sheet, and broil for about 45 minutes or until very soft when pressed and the skin is blistered and black. Cool.

2. Scoop out the flesh into a colander. Drain and press out the juices. Chop finely and stir in the remaining ingredients. Chill before serving.

Per ¼ cup: Calories 47, Protein 0 g, Carbohydrates 5 g, Fat 2 g

Variation:
• For **Israeli Eggplant Caviar**, add 3 to 4 tablespoons minced fresh parsley, diced green bell peppers, and scallions.

Mashed Eggplant Salad
with Olive Oil and Lemon

Makes 4 servings

This straightforward salad is a delectable way to serve eggplant. For extra zip, try the variations below.

1 pound eggplants
3 tablespoons extra-virgin olive oil
3 tablespoons fresh lemon juice
Salt

1. Prick the eggplants all over with a fork, and place on a dry baking sheet. Broil for about 45 minutes or until very soft when pressed and the skin is blistered and black. Cool.

2. Scoop out the flesh into a colander. Drain and press out the juices. Chop finely and stir in the remaining ingredients. Chill before serving.

Per serving: Calories 123, Protein 1 g, Carbohydrates 8 g, Fat 9 g

Variations:
• For **Syrian Mashed Eggplant Salad**, add ¼ teaspoon crushed garlic and 1 to 2 teaspoons dried spearmint.

• For **Moroccan Mashed Eggplant Salad**, add 1 teaspoon ground cumin and a pinch of cayenne pepper.

Vegetable Salads

Roasted Eggplant and Pepper Salad

Makes 6 to 8 servings

A healthful salad of cooked, chilled vegetables steeped in an awesome dressing.

1½ pounds eggplants
2 red bell peppers
2 tablespoons extra-virgin olive oil
1 teaspoon cumin
1 teaspoon paprika
¼ to ½ teaspoon crushed garlic
Good pinch of cayenne pepper
½ cup water
2 tablespoons fresh lemon juice
Salt

1. Prick the eggplants all over with a fork. Place the eggplants and whole peppers on a dry baking sheet, and broil for 30 minutes, turning once or twice. Remove the peppers and place them in a pot with a tight fitting lid. (The steam will soften and loosen the skins.) Broil the eggplants for another 15 minutes or until very soft when pressed and the skin is blistered and black. Cool.

2. When the peppers are cool enough to handle, peel off the skin using your hands, and remove the stem, ribs, and seeds. Cut into ¾-inch pieces.

3. When the eggplant is cool enough to handle, scoop out the flesh into a colander. Drain and press out the juices, and chop coarsely.

4. Heat the oil in a skillet. Add the cumin, paprika, garlic, and cayenne. Stir over low heat for 30 seconds. Remove from the heat and stir in the water, lemon juice, and salt. Add the eggplants and peppers, and simmer for 10 to 15 minutes, stirring often, until the liquid has been absorbed. Serve cold.

Per serving: Calories 67, Protein 1 g, Carbohydrates 7 g, Fat 4 g

Vegetable Salads

Sweet and Sour Eggplant and Pepper Salad

Makes 6 to 8 servings

Prosaic ingredients form a luscious, saucy salad that is practically addictive.

1½ pounds eggplants
2 red bell peppers
2 tablespoons extra-virgin olive oil
1 teaspoon crushed garlic
½ cup wine vinegar
1½ to 2 tablespoons sugar
Salt and cayenne pepper

1. Prick the eggplants all over with a fork. Place the eggplants and whole peppers on a dry baking sheet, and broil for 30 minutes, turning once or twice. Remove the peppers and place them in a pot with a tight fitting lid. (The steam will soften and loosen the skins.) Broil the eggplants for another 15 minutes or until very soft when pressed and the skin is blistered and black. Cool.

2. When the peppers are cool enough to handle, peel off the skin using your hands, and remove the stem, ribs, and seeds. Cut into ¾-inch pieces.

3. When the eggplant is cool enough to handle, scoop out the flesh into a colander. Drain and press out the juices. Coarsely chop.

4. Heat the oil in a skillet. Add the garlic and sauté over low heat for 30 seconds. Remove from the heat and stir in the vinegar, sugar, salt, and cayenne pepper. Stir well and bring to a boil. Add the eggplants and peppers, and simmer for 10 to 15 minutes, stirring often, until the liquid has been absorbed. Serve cold.

Per serving: Calories 79, Protein 1 g, Carbohydrates 11 g, Fat 4 g

Vegetable Salads

Caponata
(Italian Cold Eggplant Salad)

Makes 6 to 8 servings

Caponata makes an ideal first course or buffet salad, or a wonderful topping for pasta or rice.

2 pounds eggplants, peeled and cubed
¼ cup extra-virgin olive oil
1 large onion, chopped
½ teaspoon crushed garlic
4 ripe tomatoes, peeled and chopped
3 stalks celery, sliced or chopped
½ cup pitted green olives, cut lengthwise into quarters
4 to 6 tablespoons wine vinegar
1½ to 3 tablespoons sugar
2 tablespoons capers, rinsed and squeezed
Salt and pepper

1. Place the eggplant in a colander, and sprinkle generously with salt. Put a plate on top of the eggplant and a weight (such as a pan of water) on the plate. Let it sit for 1 hour. Then rinse the eggplant and dry gently with a clean tea towel.

2. Heat the oil in a large skillet, pan, or Dutch oven. Add the onion and sauté until soft. Add the garlic and sauté for 1 minute. Add the eggplant, tomatoes, celery, olives, vinegar, sugar, capers, salt, and pepper. (Start with the smaller amounts of vinegar and sugar, and add more to taste at the end.) Bring to a boil. Reduce the heat slightly and simmer, stirring often, until the tomatoes have cooked down to a thick sauce, about 25 to 30 minutes. Chill thoroughly before serving.

Per serving: Calories 153, Protein 1 g, Carbohydrates 18 g, Fat 8 g

Vegetable Salads

Cold Mushroom Salad
with Cilantro and Cumin

Makes 6 to 8 servings

These mushrooms, cooked in a light marinade, chilled, and dressed with cilantro, are absolutely splendid.

1 pound fresh mushrooms
¼ cup extra-virgin olive oil
2 teaspoons cumin
½ teaspoon crushed garlic
Salt and cayenne pepper
2 tablespoons fresh lemon juice
Chopped fresh cilantro

1. Wash the mushrooms. Cut them in half or quarters, or leave whole if very small.

2. Heat the oil in a large skillet. Add the mushrooms, cumin, garlic, salt, and cayenne, and stir well. Add the lemon juice and cook over medium-low heat for about 10 minutes. Chill thoroughly. Stir in the cilantro just before serving.

Per servin   alories 85, Protein 1 g, Carbohydrates 3 g, Fat 8 g

Vegetable Salads

Zucchini and Olive Salad

Makes 6 to 8 servings

Black olives and garlic complement shy zucchini, bringing out its subtle charms.

1½ pounds zucchini
2 tablespoons extra-virgin olive oil
2 tablespoons fresh lemon juice
8 black olives, chopped
1 teaspoon ground coriander
½ teaspoon crushed garlic
Salt

1. Trim the zucchini and cut it into large chunks. Steam or boil until soft. Drain, cool, and press gently in a colander to squeeze out the extra water.

2. Chop the zucchini with a knife, then transfer to a bowl and mash with a fork. Add the remaining ingredients and mix well. Chill thoroughly before serving.

Per serving: Calories 54, Protein 1 g, Carbohydrates 3 g, Fat 4 g

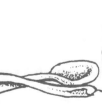

Vegetable Salads

Mashed Zucchini Salad

Makes 6 to 8 servings

A light salad kissed with exotic spices.

1½ pounds zucchini
2 tablespoons extra-virgin olive oil
2 tablespoons fresh lemon juice
1 teaspoon ground coriander
1 teaspoon ground caraway
½ teaspoon crushed garlic
Salt and pepper
Good pinch of cayenne pepper

1. Trim the zucchini and cut it into large chunks. Steam or boil until soft. Drain, cool, and press gently in a colander to squeeze out the extra water.

2. Chop the zucchini with a knife, then transfer to a bowl and mash with a fork. Add the remaining ingredients and mix well. Chill thoroughly before serving.

Per serving: Calories 49, Protein 1 g, Carbohydrates 3 g, Fat 4 g

Vegetable Salads

Marinated Zucchini

Makes 4 to 6 servings

The zucchini in this recipe is uncooked, but it acquires a tender, almost cooked texture as it marinates.

1 pound zucchini (about 4 medium or 3 large), very thinly
    sliced on the diagonal
¼ cup fresh lemon juice
1 tablespoon extra-virgin olive oil
½ teaspoon crushed garlic
Salt and pepper
Chopped fresh basil or parsley

Place the zucchini in a bowl, and toss with the lemon juice, olive oil, garlic, salt, and pepper. Cover and refrigerate 4 to 8 hours, tossing occasionally. Toss with the herbs just before serving.

Per serving: Calories 40, Protein 1 g, Carbohydrates 3 g, Fat 2 g

Vegetable Salads

Bean & Tofu Salads

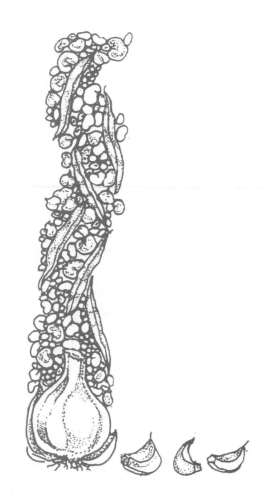

Humble Chick-Pea Salad

Makes 4 servings

This dish is sometimes called "bead hummus," because the shimmering chick-peas are reminiscent of precious jewels.

2 cups drained cooked chick-peas
2 tablespoons extra-virgin olive oil
2 tablespoons fresh lemon juice
½ teaspoon ground cumin
Pinch of cayenne pepper
¼ teaspoon crushed garlic
2 tablespoons minced fresh parsley
Salt

Place the beans in a large bowl. Add the remaining ingredients and toss gently. Chill before serving.

Per serving: Calories 196, Protein 6 g, Carbohydrates 23 g, Fat 7 g

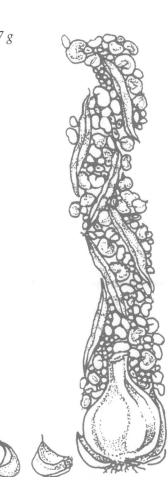

Bean & Tofu Salads

Warm Chick-Pea Salad

Makes 6 servings

Hearty chick-peas tossed with a mix of crunchy vegetables and a tangy dressing make a satisfying entree or side dish.

6 cups drained cooked chick-peas
1 green or red bell pepper, chopped
½ cup chopped fresh parsley
4 scallions, chopped
4 red radishes, sliced
¼ cup fresh lemon juice
3 tablespoons extra-virgin olive oil
2 tablespoons wine vinegar
1 tablespoon Dijon mustard
¼ teaspoon crushed garlic
Salt and pepper

1. Warm the beans, then toss with the bell pepper, parsley, scallions, and radishes.

2. In a separate bowl, whisk together the remaining ingredients. Pour over the chick-peas and mix thoroughly. Serve warm.

Per serving: Calories 342, Protein 13 g, Carbohydrates 48 g, Fat 9 g

Bean & Tofu Salads

Salad of Chick-Peas, Tomato, and Walnuts

Makes 4 servings

This delightful salad is a fine example of how simple ingredients often create the most memorable dishes. Serve it with a hearty whole-grain bread to dip into the flavorful dressing.

2 cups drained cooked chick-peas
1 medium tomato, chopped
¼ cup walnuts, broken into pieces
¼ cup raisins
¼ cup minced fresh parsley
2 tablespoons fresh lemon juice
1 tablespoon extra-virgin olive oil
Salt and pepper

Combine all the ingredients in a large bowl. Toss to mix well.

Per serving: Calories 248, Protein 8 g, Carbohydrates 33 g, Fat 9 g

Bean & Tofu Salads

Chick-Pea "Tuna" Salad

Makes 2 to 4 servings

For an attractive luncheon, scoop this salad onto lettuce-lined plates, garnish it with a little paprika, and surround it with fresh tomato wedges. Alternatively, spread it on whole grain bread or stuff it into whole wheat pitas with lettuce and fresh tomato slices.

2 cups drained cooked chick-peas
½ cup finely diced celery
2 tablespoons fresh lemon juice
1 tablespoon extra-virgin olive oil
1 thinly sliced scallion, or grated onion to taste
2 tablespoons minced fresh parsley (optional)
2 teaspoons well-drained pickle relish or chopped pickles
2 teaspoons brown mustard
¼ teaspoon paprika
Salt and pepper

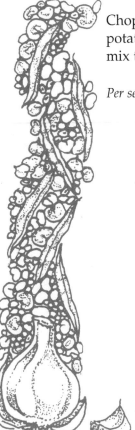

Chop the beans in a food processor, or mash them well with a potato masher or fork. Stir in the remaining ingredients, and mix thoroughly. Chill before serving.

Per serving: Calories 234, Protein 8 g, Carbohydrates 33 g, Fat 7 g

Chick-Peas with Spinach

Makes 6 servings

The bright flavors of lemon and spearmint add a refreshing surprise to this lovely dish.

1 pound fresh spinach (stems removed)
2 tablespoons extra-virgin olive oil
1 large onion, chopped
1 teaspoon ground coriander
$\frac{1}{4}$ to $\frac{1}{2}$ teaspoon crushed garlic
Salt and pepper
3 cups drained cooked chick-peas (reserve $\frac{1}{2}$ cup of the
    cooking liquid)
2 tablespoons fresh lemon juice
1 teaspoon dried spearmint

1. Wash the spinach and pat dry in a clean tea towel. Chop finely.

2. Heat the oil in a large skillet or pot. Add the onion and coriander, and sauté until the onion is tender and golden brown. Add the spinach and garlic, and cook over medium-high heat for 5 minutes. Add the chick-peas, the $\frac{1}{2}$ cup of cooking liquid, salt, and pepper. Simmer uncovered 5 to 10 minutes or until the liquid is absorbed.

3. Stir in the lemon juice and mint. Serve warm or chilled.

Per serving: Calories 200, Protein 8 g, Carbohydrates 27 g, Fat 6 g

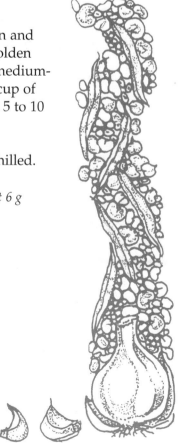

Bean & Tofu Salads

Balkan White Bean Salad

Makes 6 servings

The basic, fresh ingredients in this salad make a beautiful and enjoyable combination.

3 cups drained cooked white beans
3 to 4 tablespoons extra-virgin olive oil
2 tablespoons white wine vinegar
Salt and pepper
Minced mild onion
Minced fresh parsley
2 medium tomatoes, cut into 12 wedges
8 to 12 pitted black olives

1. Place the beans in a large bowl. Dress with the oil, vinegar, salt, and pepper.

2. Stir in the onion and parsley, and toss gently. Serve garnished with the tomatoes and olives.

Per serving: Calories 211, Protein 8 g, Carbohydrates 25 g, Fat 8 g

Bean & Tofu Salads

White Bean Salad
with Cilantro and Mint

Makes 4 to 6 servings

*Colorful and exotic, this salad makes a terrific first course, a
beautiful addition to a party buffet, or a tasty and refreshing picnic
dish. Use Great Northern beans, navy beans, or other white beans of
your choice.*

3 cups drained cooked white beans
1 cup chopped fresh cilantro, lightly packed
1 red bell pepper, finely diced
$\frac{1}{4}$ cup fresh lemon juice
$\frac{1}{4}$ cup chopped fresh mint, or 1 teaspoon dried spearmint
3 tablespoons extra-virgin olive oil
$\frac{1}{4}$ teaspoon crushed garlic
$\frac{1}{4}$ teaspoon ground cumin
Salt and pepper

Place the beans in a large bowl. Add the remaining ingredients, and toss gently but thoroughly.

Per serving: Calories 232, Protein 9 g, Carbohydrates 30 g, Fat 8 g

Bean & Tofu Salads

Grecian White Bean Salad

Makes 4 to 6 servings

A tart and spunky dressing enlivens the mild and humble white bean.

3 cups drained cooked white beans
3 tablespoons extra-virgin olive oil
3 tablespoons red wine vinegar
3 tablespoons fresh lemon juice
1 teaspoon dried oregano
½ teaspoon crushed garlic
Salt and pepper

Place the beans in a large bowl. Add the remaining ingredients, and toss gently but thoroughly.

Per serving: Calories 225, Protein 9 g, Carbohydrates 28 g, Fat 8 g

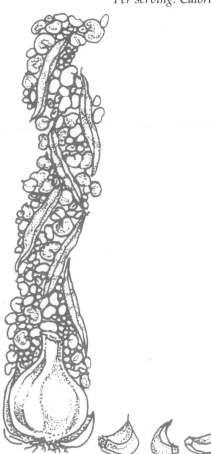

Bean & Tofu Salads

Turkish-Style White Beans and Tomatoes

Makes 8 servings

Cooked vegetables form a rich, enchanting sauce that melds poetically with delicate white beans and the spark of fresh herbs.

¼ cup extra-virgin olive oil
2 large onions, chopped
1 teaspoon crushed garlic
6 ripe tomatoes, peeled and chopped
Salt and pepper
6 cups drained cooked white beans (reserve 1 cup of the
    cooking liquid)
1 teaspoon paprika
Pinch of cayenne pepper
¼ cup minced fresh parsley or cilantro
Lemon wedges (optional)

1. Heat the oil in a large pot or Dutch oven. Add the onions and sauté until tender and starting to brown. Add the garlic and sauté for 1 minute. Stir in the tomatoes, salt, and pepper, and simmer, uncovered, for 30 minutes, stirring often.

2. Add the beans and the cooking liquid, paprika, and cayenne. Simmer for 20 minutes, then chill thoroughly. Stir in the parsley or cilantro just before serving. Serve with lemon wedges on the side, if desired.

Per serving: Calories 279, Protein 12 g, Carbohydrates 41 g, Fat 7 g

Bean & Tofu Salads

Lentil Salad

Makes 6 to 8 servings

A high-protein salad that makes a substantial entrée any time of the year.

4 cups drained cooked lentils
¼ cup extra-virgin olive oil
¼ cup fresh lemon juice
Minced fresh parsley
½ teaspoon crushed garlic
½ teaspoon ground cumin (optional)
Salt and pepper

Place the lentils in a large bowl. Add the remaining ingredients and toss gently. Chill before serving.

Per serving: Calories 202, Protein 9 g, Carbohydrates 24 g, Fat 8 g

Bean & Tofu Salads

Lentil and Bulgur Salad

Makes 6 servings

Lentils and bulgur join forces to create a power-packed salad that's certain to appease even the hungriest appetite.

1 cup dried lentils, rinsed and drained
4 cups water
1 large onion, finely chopped
¼ cup extra-virgin olive oil
½ cup bulgur
½ cup minced fresh parsley
Salt and pepper
Lemon wedges

1. Place the lentils and water in a large, heavy saucepan or Dutch oven, and bring to a boil. Moderate the heat, cover, and simmer for 20 minutes.

2. Meanwhile, sauté the onion in the olive oil until tender and well browned. Add to the lentils. Stir in the bulgur, cover, and simmer, stirring occasionally, until the bulgur is tender and the water is absorbed, about 25 to 30 minutes longer.

3. Remove from the heat and stir in the parsley. Season with salt and pepper. Cool, then refrigerate until thoroughly chilled. Serve with lemon wedges on the side.

Per serving: Calories 223, Protein 8 g, Carbohydrates 27 g, Fat 9 g

Tip:
• If the mixture starts sticking to or burning on the bottom of the pot, reduce the heat or slip a heat diffuser under the pot.

Variation:
• For **Lentil and Quinoa Salad**, replace the bulgur with ½ cup quinoa, rinsed well and drained.

Bean & Tofu Salads

Three Bean Salad

Makes 7 cups (about 10 servings)

What deli would be complete without the most beloved bean salad of all time? Here is a delicious version of this triple-header delight.

2 cups drained cooked chick-peas
2 cups drained cooked red kidney beans
2 cups cooked green beans, cut into 1-inch lengths
½ cup julienned red onions
½ cup sliced black olives
¼ cup extra-virgin olive oil
¼ cup fresh lemon juice or wine vinegar
¼ cup pure maple syrup or brown rice syrup
Salt

1. Combine the beans, onions, and olives in a large bowl.

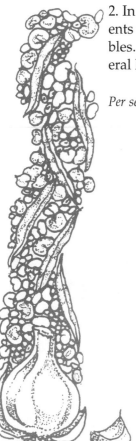

2. In a separate bowl, whisk together the remaining ingredients until well blended, and pour over the beans and vegetables. Toss gently. Cover and marinate in the refrigerator several hours or overnight.

Per serving: Calories 190, Protein 6 g, Carbohydrates 25 g, Fat 7 g

Egyptian Black-Eyed Pea Salad

Makes 6 to 8 servings

Mild-tasting black-eyed peas are paired with zesty seasonings for an out-of-the-ordinary bean salad.

4 cups drained cooked black-eyed peas
1 red onion, chopped, or 1/2 teaspoon crushed garlic
1/4 cup extra-virgin olive oil
3 to 4 tablespoons fresh lemon juice
Minced fresh parsley
1/2 teaspoon ground cumin (optional)
Cayenne pepper

Place the peas in a large bowl. Add the remaining ingredients and toss gently. Chill before serving.

Per serving: Calories 192, Protein 7 g, Carbohydrates 23 g, Fat 8 g

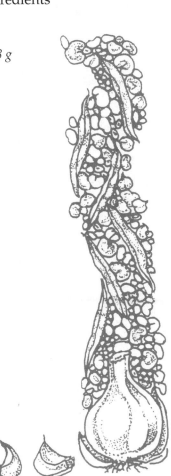

Bean & Tofu Salads

Boneless Chickenless Chicken Salad

Makes 4 cups (about 6 servings)

This salad is a great pretender — it has all the ingredients that make a great "chicken" salad, without the bird! Serve it on a bed of fresh, crisp greens or as a hearty sandwich filling.

1 pound extra-firm regular tofu, rinsed and patted dry
1 cup water
$\frac{1}{4}$ cup natural soy sauce
1 cup Deli Dressing, p. 122, or vegan mayonnaise
$1\frac{1}{2}$ to 2 teaspoons Dijon mustard
$\frac{1}{2}$ cup finely diced celery
$\frac{1}{2}$ cup finely diced bell pepper (green or red)
Thinly sliced scallions or grated onion (optional)

1. Oil a baking sheet or coat it with nonstick cooking spray, and set aside. Cut the tofu into $\frac{1}{4}$-inch-thick slices. Place in two shallow dishes, large enough to fit the tofu in a single layer.

2. Combine the water and soy sauce, and pour over the tofu. Let marinate 15 to 30 minutes.

3. Preheat the oven to 400°F. Remove the tofu from the marinade, and place in a single layer on the baking sheet. Bake until a deep, golden brown and the surface is dry, about 30 minutes.

4. Allow the tofu to cool until it can be easily handled, then slice it into very thin strips or shreds. Transfer to a bowl with the vegetables, and add thinly sliced scallions or grated onion, if desired.

5. Stir together the dressing and mustard. Add just enough to the salad to moisten it to your liking. Toss gently until everything is evenly coated. Chill before serving.

Per serving: Calories 149, Protein 9 g, Carbohydrates 4 g, Fat 10 g

Variation:
• For **Southern-Style Chickenless Salad**, omit the bell pepper and scallions and add ½ cup chopped pecans.

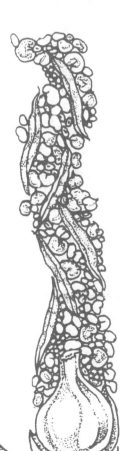

Bean & Tofu Salads

Tempeh Pecan Salad

Makes 4 servings

Southern-style chicken salad without the chicken!

One 8-ounce package frozen tempeh, thawed
½ cup Deli Dressing, p. 122, or vegan mayonnaise
½ cup chopped pecans
½ cup finely diced celery
2 tablespoons finely minced red onion (optional)
2 tablespoons minced fresh parsley
Salt and pepper

Steam the tempeh for 20 minutes, then cool. Cut into ¼-inch cubes, and place in a bowl. Add the remaining ingredients and mix gently. Chill thoroughly before serving.

Per serving: Calories 272, Protein 13 g, Carbohydrates 15 g, Fat 18 g

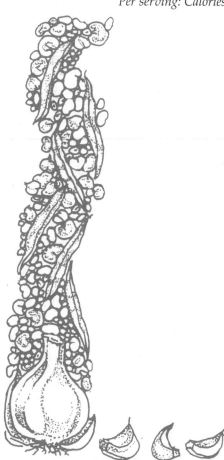

Bean & Tofu Salads

Cottage Salad

Makes 4 to 6 servings

Early spring vegetables were a refreshing change from the root vegetables and cabbage eaten during winter by Eastern Europeans. The vegetables were crisp, flavorful, and special because they were prepared fresh instead of from storage or pickled. Although this salad is traditionally made with dairy products, this creamy, dairy-free version tastes incredibly authentic. Serve it on a bed of lettuce with bread or crackers and red ripe tomatoes on the side to add a complement of "new world" flavors.

1 pound firm regular tofu, rinsed
2 cups diced English cucumber
1 cup Sour Dressing, p. 123
1 cup red radishes, sliced into half moons
½ cup thinly sliced scallions
1 teaspoon salt
1 teaspoon dried dill
Pepper

1. Place the tofu in a saucepan with enough water to cover, and bring to a boil. Reduce the heat, cover, and simmer for 10 minutes. Drain and place in a bowl of ice water to cool. Drain well and press gently to remove any excess water. Pat dry. Transfer to a bowl and mash using your hands.

2. Combine the remaining ingredients with the tofu, and mix gently but thoroughly. Adjust the salt and pepper to taste. Chill thoroughly before serving.

Per serving: Calories 165, Protein 11 g, Carbohydrates 8 g, Fat 9 g

Tip:
• For a terrific sandwich, stuff the salad into pita pockets or roll it in lavosh, chapatis, or whole wheat tortillas.

Bean & Tofu Salads

Curried Tofu Salad

Makes 6 servings

Bland tofu takes on an intriguing new identity in this sweet and spicy dish.

1 pound firm regular tofu, rinsed
½ cup Deli Dressing, p. 122, or vegan mayonnaise
1 to 2 teaspoons curry powder
One 16-ounce can unsweetened crushed pineapple, drained
¼ cup raisins

1. Place the tofu in a saucepan with enough water to cover, and bring to a boil. Reduce the heat, cover, and simmer for 10 minutes. Drain and place in a bowl of ice water to cool. Drain well and press gently to remove any excess water. Pat dry and cut into ¼-inch cubes. Transfer to a bowl.

2. Combine the mayonnaise and curry powder in a large bowl. Stir in the pineapple and raisins, then carefully fold in the tofu cubes and mix gently. Chill thoroughly before serving.

Per serving: Calories 162, Protein 7 g, Carbohydrates 17 g, Fat 6 g

Grain, Potato & Pasta Salads

Tabooli

Makes 6 servings

This recipe was preserved by Jews who emigrated to Egypt and the Americas around the turn of the nineteenth century. It is more wheaty than the very green Middle Eastern-style salad of the same name. Although it doesn't take much time or effort to prepare, it must marinate in the refrigerator for several hours to properly soften the bulgur.

1 cup bulgur
1½ cups boiling water
1 teaspoon salt
¼ cup fresh lemon juice
¼ cup extra-virgin olive oil
1 cup minced fresh parsley
1 ripe tomato, diced (optional)
4 scallions, thinly sliced
¼ cup chopped fresh mint, or 2 teaspoons dried spearmint
½ teaspoon crushed garlic

1. Place the bulgur in a heat-proof mixing bowl. Dissolve the salt in the boiling water, and pour over the bulgur. Mix well, cover, and let sit for 30 minutes.

2. Combine the lemon juice and olive oil, and add to the bulgur. Stir in the parsley, tomato, scallions, mint, and garlic, and mix well. Cover tightly and marinate the salad in the refrigerator for 4 to 12 hours.

Per serving: Calories 171, Protein 3 g, Carbohydrates 19 g, Fat 9 g

Grain, Potato & Pasta Salads

Variations:
• For **Middle Eastern-Style Tabooli**, add 1 extra cup of parsley and 1 cup diced English cucumbers.

• For **Quinoa Tabooli**, replace the bulgur with 1 cup quinoa. Place the quinoa in a fine mesh strainer, and rinse well under running water, stirring it with your fingers. Place in a pot with 2 cups water and the salt, and bring to a boil. Reduce the heat, cover, and simmer for 15 minutes or until tender. Remove from the heat, cover, and let rest for 10 minutes. Fluff and proceed with step 2 of the directions.

Grain, Potato & Pasta Salads

Cracked Wheat and Nut Salad

Makes 8 to 10 servings

A satisfying grain salad with phenomenal texture and flavor.

2 cups bulgur
1½ teaspoons salt
3 cups boiling water
¼ cup extra-virgin olive oil
2 tablespoons light molasses
¼ cup fresh lemon juice
4 tablespoons tomato paste
¾ teaspoon ground cumin
¾ teaspoon ground coriander
¼ teaspoon ground allspice
¼ teaspoon cayenne pepper
1 cup minced fresh parsley or cilantro
1 cup coarsely chopped walnuts
½ cup coarsely chopped pistachios or hazelnuts
¼ cup pignolia nuts, lightly toasted

1. Place the bulgur in a heat-proof mixing bowl. Dissolve the salt in the boiling water, and pour over the bulgur. Mix well, cover, and let sit for 30 minutes.

Grain, Potato & Pasta Salads

2. In a small bowl, whisk together the olive oil and molasses. Beat in the lemon juice, tomato paste, cumin, coriander, allspice, and cayenne. Pour over the bulgur and mix well. Add the parsley or cilantro and nuts, and mix well. Cover tightly and marinate in the refrigerator for 4 to 12 hours.

Per serving: Calories 348, Protein 9 g, Carbohydrates 35 g, Fat 18 g

Variation:
• For **Quinoa and Nut Salad**, replace the bulgur with 2 cups quinoa. Place the quinoa in a fine mesh strainer, and rinse well under running water, stirring it with your fingers. Place in a large pot with 4 cups water and the salt, and bring to a boil. Reduce the heat, cover, and simmer for about 15 minutes or until tender. Remove from the heat, cover, and let rest for 10 minutes. Fluff and proceed with step 2 of the directions.

Grain, Potato & Pasta Salads

Rice and Bean Salad
with Tomatoes, Olives, and Capers

Makes 8 to 10 servings

A rich and hearty dish with a Mediterranean twist.

4 cups water
2 cups brown rice, or a mixture of brown and wild rice
¼ cup extra-virgin olive oil
3 tablespoons white wine vinegar
Salt and pepper
3 cups drained cooked chick-peas
12 small cherry tomatoes, cut in quarters
12 to 16 pitted black olives, cut in quarters lengthwise
3 tablespoons capers, rinsed and squeezed

1. Bring the water to a boil. Add the rice and a pinch of salt. Cover, reduce the heat to low, and simmer for 1 hour. Remove from the heat and let sit, covered, for 10 minutes.

2. Transfer the rice to a large bowl. While still hot, dress the rice with oil, vinegar, salt, and pepper. Add the remaining ingredients and mix well. Serve warm or thoroughly chilled.

Per serving: Calories 275, Protein 7 g, Carbohydrates 42 g, Fat 7 g

Grain, Potato & Pasta Salads

Rice, Zucchini, and Corn Salad

Makes 6 servings

A chewy and beautiful main dish salad. Serve with brightly colorful vegetables on the side, such as carrots, beets, or tomatoes.

3 cups cooked brown rice or a mixture of brown and wild rice
1 pound small zucchini, cut in half lengthwise and sliced into
    half moons
2 cups cooked corn kernels
1/4 cup thinly sliced scallions
1/4 cup extra-virgin olive oil
3 tablespoons fresh lemon juice
2 teaspoons Dijon mustard
2 teaspoons dried dill
1/2 teaspoon salt

Combine the rice, zucchini, corn, and scallions in a large bowl. Whisk together the remaining ingredients. Pour over the rice and vegetables, and toss well. Serve warm or thoroughly chilled.

Per serving: Calories 255, Protein 4 g, Carbohydrates 38 g, Fat 9 g

Curried Grain and Apple Salad

Makes 6 servings

This sweet and spicy fruit and vegetable salad makes a very special entrée. Serve it with soup and dark leafy greens or coleslaw for an unbeatable and filling meal.

3 cups cooked grain (such brown rice, wild rice, bulgur, or
     barley, or a combination)
2 Granny Smith apples, diced
½ cup coarsely chopped walnuts
½ cup chopped pitted dates
2 stalks celery, sliced and diced
1 small carrot, scraped and finely chopped (optional)
½ cup Deli Dressing, p. 122, or vegan mayonnaise
1 to 2 teaspoons curry powder
Salt and pepper

1. Combine the grain, apples, walnuts, dates, celery, and carrot in a large bowl.

2. In a small bowl, whisk together the Deli Dressing and curry powder. Add to the salad, using just enough to moisten. Season with salt and pepper, and toss well. Serve chilled.

Per serving: Calories 295, Protein 6 g, Carbohydrates 45 g, Fat 10 g

Variations:
• Omit the carrot and add ½ cup seedless grapes.

• Use ⅓ cup lightly toasted sunflower or pumpkin seeds in place of the walnuts.

Grain, Potato & Pasta Salads

Citrus Fruit and Grain Salad

Makes 6 servings

Citrus fruit and cooked grain make a surprisingly exquisite combination.

4 cups cooked grain (such as brown rice, wild rice, bulgur,
    quinoa, or barley, or a combination)
2 navel oranges, peeled and chopped
1/2 cup minced fresh parsley
1/3 cup raisins
1/4 cup extra-virgin olive oil
3 tablespoons fresh lemon juice
1 tablespoon wine vinegar
2 teaspoons Dijon mustard
Salt and pepper

1. Combine the grain, oranges, parsley, and raisins in a large bowl.

2. In a small bowl, whisk together the oil, lemon juice, vinegar, and mustard. Pour over the rice and fruit, and toss well. Season with salt and pepper, and toss again. Serve chilled.

Per serving: Calories 285, Protein 4 g, Carbohydrates 45 g, Fat 9 g

Deli Potato Salad

Makes 6 to 8 servings

One of the best!

6 medium thin-skinned potatoes (red, white, or gold)
1⅓ cups Deli Dressing, p. 122, or vegan mayonnaise
2 to 3 tablespoons finely minced or grated onion
1 tablespoon white wine vinegar
1 tablespoon prepared yellow mustard
1 teaspoon celery seeds
Salt and pepper
Paprika

1. Cut the potatoes into cubes or bite-size chunks, making about 6 cups. Steam until tender. Set aside to cool slightly.

2. Combine the dressing, onion, vinegar, mustard, and celery seeds in a large glass or ceramic mixing bowl. Mix well.

3. Add the potatoes, salt, and pepper to the dressing, and toss gently. Chill thoroughly. Garnish with paprika just before serving.

Per serving: Calories 206, Protein 5 g, Carbohydrates 26 g, Fat 10 g

Grandma's Potato Salad

Makes 6 to 8 servings

Where the taste of tradition begins.

6 medium thin-skinned potatoes (red, white, or gold)
1⅓ cups Deli Dressing, p. 122, or vegan mayonnaise
2 to 3 tablespoons minced red onion
2 tablespoons white wine vinegar
1 red bell pepper, diced
½ cup diced celery
Salt and pepper
Chopped fresh parsley

1. Cut the potatoes into cubes or bite-size chunks, making about 6 cups. Steam until tender, then set aside to cool slightly.

2. Combine the dressing, onion, and vinegar in a large glass or ceramic mixing bowl. Mix well.

3. Add the cubed potatoes, red bell pepper, celery, salt, and pepper to the dressing, and toss gently. Chill thoroughly. Garnish with parsley just before serving.

Per serving: Calories 210, Protein 5 g, Carbohydrates 26 g, Fat 10 g

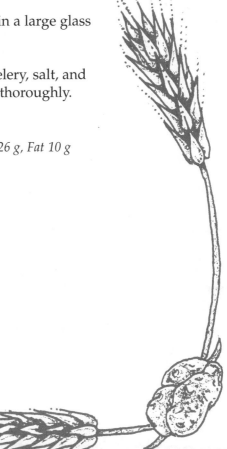

Grain, Potato & Pasta Salads

Potato Salad
with Sesame-Tarragon Dressing

Makes 6 to 8 servings

Not a run-of-the-mill potato salad. Sizzle your taste buds and excite your friends and family with the zing of this unique dish.

6 medium thin-skinned potatoes (red, white, or gold)
⅓ cup extra-virgin olive oil
⅓ cup fresh lemon juice
2 tablespoons tahini
1 tablespoon dried tarragon
2 teaspoons Dijon mustard
½ teaspoon salt
Bottled hot pepper sauce
½ cup minced red onion
2 tablespoons minced fresh parsley

1. Cut the potatoes into cubes or bite-size chunks, making about 6 cups. Steam until tender, then set aside to cool slightly.

2. In a large bowl, whisk together the oil, lemon juice, tahini, tarragon, mustard, salt, and hot pepper sauce to taste. Add the potatoes, onion, and parsley, and toss gently. Serve warm or thoroughly chilled.

Per serving: Calories 218, Protein 2 g, Carbohydrates 26 g, Fat 12 g

Grain, Potato & Pasta Salads

Vinaigrette Potato Salad

Makes 6 to 8 servings

It's true — there's absolutely no law that mandates potato salads be laden with mayonnaise! Try this vinaigrette-style potato salad for a welcome change.

6 medium thin-skinned potatoes (red, white, or gold)
⅓ cup extra-virgin olive oil
2 tablespoons wine vinegar or cider vinegar
Salt and pepper
½ cup minced red onion, or 6 thinly sliced scallions
3 tablespoons minced fresh parsley

1. Cut the potatoes into cubes or bite-size chunks, making about 6 cups. Steam until tender. Transfer to a bowl.

2. Whisk together the oil, vinegar, salt, and pepper. Pour over the warm potatoes. Add the onion or scallions and parsley, and mix gently. Serve warm or thoroughly chilled.

Per serving: Calories 189, Protein 1 g, Carbohydrates 24 g, Fat 9 g

Variation:
• Beat into the dressing 1 teaspoon dry mustard, and add to the salad 1 to 2 small pickles, chopped.

Grain, Potato & Pasta Salads

New Potato Salad
with Olives and Capers

Makes 6 servings

The piquant additions of lemon juice, olives, and capers put this wonderful potato salad in a class of its own.

1 pound new potatoes
¼ cup fresh lemon juice
¼ cup extra-virgin olive oil
Salt and pepper
18 to 20 pitted black or green olives, chopped
2 tablespoons capers, rinsed and squeezed
4 to 6 scallions, thinly sliced

1. Boil the potatoes in salted water until tender. Cut in half, if small, or quarters, if large.

2. Dress the potatoes with the lemon juice, olive oil, salt, and pepper. Toss gently. Add the remaining ingredients and mix well. Serve warm or thoroughly chilled.

Per serving: Calories 166, Protein 1 g, Carbohydrates 17 g, Fat 11 g

Grain, Potato & Pasta Salads

Tunisian Potato Salad

Makes 6 servings

*Commonplace potato salad springs to life with the timeless addition
of a few simple seasonings.*

1 pound new potatoes
¼ cup fresh lemon juice
¼ cup extra-virgin olive oil
1 teaspoon ground cumin
½ teaspoon paprika
Good pinch of cayenne pepper
Salt

Boil the potatoes in salted water until tender. Cut in half, if
small, or quarters, if large. Dress with the remaining ingredients, and toss gently. Serve warm or thoroughly chilled.

Per serving: Calories 147, Protein 1 g, Carbohydrates 16 g, Fat 9 g

Mashed Carrot and Potato Salad

Makes 8 servings

An unusual, attractive, and remarkably delectable treatment for potatoes and carrots.

1 pound potatoes
1 pound carrots
¼ cup extra-virgin olive oil
2 to 4 tablespoons fresh lemon juice
1 teaspoon paprika
½ teaspoon ground cumin
½ teaspoon crushed garlic
Salt
Good pinch of cayenne pepper

1. Peel the potatoes. Trim and scrape the carrots. Cut into large chunks and boil in lightly salted water until very tender, about 20 minutes. Drain and cool. Chop with a knife, then transfer to a bowl and mash with a potato masher or fork.

2. In a separate bowl, whisk together the remaining ingredients. Pour over the potatoes and carrots, and mix well. Chill thoroughly before serving.

Per serving: Calories 134, Protein 1 g, Carbohydrates 17 g, Fat 7 g

Grain, Potato & Pasta Salads

Noodles in Peanut Sauce

Makes 8 servings

Enticing, enchanting, and irresistible!

½ cup peanut butter
2 tablespoons natural soy sauce
2 tablespoons toasted sesame oil
1 tablespoon rice vinegar
1 teaspoon pure maple syrup or rice syrup
½ teaspoon ground ginger
½ teaspoon crushed garlic
Cayenne pepper
Water
12 ounces thin whole wheat spaghetti
Thinly sliced scallions (optional)
Toasted sesame seeds (optional)

1. In a large bowl, combine the peanut butter, soy sauce, oil, vinegar, syrup, ginger, garlic, and cayenne. Stir vigorously until smooth and well combined. Gradually whisk in enough water to make a pourable sauce, about 1 cup.

2. Boil the noodles in lightly salted water. Drain well, rinse under cold water to cool, then drain again.

3. Add the noodles to the bowl with the sauce, and toss until evenly coated. Chill thoroughly before serving. The noodles will absorb any excess sauce as they chill. Garnish with scallions and/or toasted sesame seeds, if desired.

Per serving: Calories 187, Protein 7 g, Carbohydrates 16 g, Fat 11 g

Grain, Potato & Pasta Salads

Cold Sesame Noodles and Vegetables

Makes 6 to 8 servings

Colorful vegetables and thin noodles luxuriate in an exciting, Asian-inspired dressing.

12 ounces whole wheat spaghetti
2 cups diagonally sliced carrots
2 cups broccoli florets
3 scallions, thinly sliced
¼ cup rice vinegar
¼ cup toasted sesame oil
3 tablespoons natural soy sauce
2 tablespoons sugar
1 teaspoon ground ginger
¼ teaspoon crushed garlic
¼ teaspoon salt
Cayenne pepper
Toasted sesame seeds

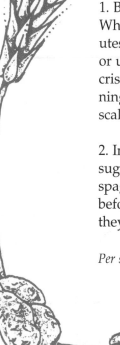

1. Bring a large pot of water to a boil, and add the spaghetti. When the water returns to a boil, add the carrots. After 6 minutes, add the broccoli florets and cook about 3 minutes longer, or until the spaghetti is done and the vegetables are tender-crisp. Drain and immediately cool by rinsing under cold running water; drain again. Transfer to a large bowl, and add the scallions.

2. In a small bowl, whisk together the vinegar, oil, soy sauce, sugar, ginger, garlic, salt, and cayenne pepper. Pour over the spaghetti and vegetables, and toss gently. Chill thoroughly before serving. The noodles will absorb any excess sauce as they chill. Garnish with toasted sesame seeds.

Per serving: Calories 174, Protein 4 g, Carbohydrates 21 g, Fat 7 g

Grain, Potato & Pasta Salads

Cold Pasta with Tomato Sauce

Makes 6 servings

Sophisticated and sensational!

3 tablespoons extra-virgin olive oil
1 teaspoon crushed garlic
4 large ripe tomatoes, peeled and chopped, or one 28-ounce
    can tomatoes, drained and chopped
2 tablespoons wine vinegar
1 tablespoon sugar
Salt
Good pinch of cayenne pepper
1 bunch fresh parsley or basil, chopped
12 ounces thin spaghetti

1. Heat 2 tablespoons of the olive oil in a large skillet. Add the garlic and sauté for 30 seconds. Stir in the tomatoes, vinegar, sugar, salt, and cayenne, and simmer until thick, about 25 to 30 minutes. Remove from the heat and stir in the parsley or basil.

2. Cook the pasta in boiling salted water until tender. Drain and toss with the remaining 1 tablespoon oil, then toss with the tomato sauce. Serve at room temperature or thoroughly chilled.

Per serving: Calories 168, Protein 4 g, Carbohydrates 23 g, Fat 7 g

Pasta with Sour Plum Sauce

Makes 6 to 8 servings

This simple but electrifying dish requires no added salt. The naturally salty plum paste adds both salt seasonings and a tart, compelling sour flavor.

1 pound whole wheat elbow macaroni or other short, whole
    wheat pasta
⅓ cup extra-virgin olive oil
4 tablespoons umeboshi plum paste
2 to 3 teaspoons crushed garlic
¾ cup minced fresh parsley
Pepper

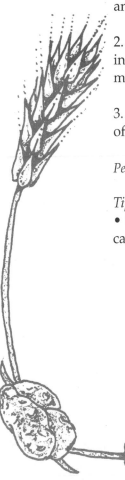

1. Cook the pasta in boiling salted water until tender. Drain and transfer to a large bowl.

2. While the pasta is cooking, prepare the sauce. Heat the oil in a small pot or skillet. Add the garlic and sauté for 1 minute. Add the plum paste and stir until almost melted.

3. Pour the sauce over the pasta, add the parsley and plenty of pepper, and mix well. Serve warm or thoroughly chilled.

Per serving: Calories 216, Protein 4 g, Carbohydrates 26 g, Fat 9 g

Tip:
• Umeboshi plum paste is a salty Japanese condiment that can be found in the macrobiotic section of natural food stores.

Grain, Potato & Pasta Salads

Spreads

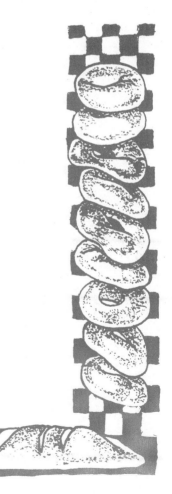

Green Bean and Walnut Pâté

Makes about 2 cups

Serve this classic deli spread on a bed of lettuce garnished with tomatoes or as a spread for matzo, crackers, or bread. You can feel good about the walnuts in this recipe as they are an excellent source of essential fatty acids.

1 tablespoon extra-virgin olive oil
1 large onion, diced
2 cups steamed green beans, cooled and coarsely chopped
½ pound firm regular tofu, rinsed
1 cup chopped walnuts
Pinch of ground allspice
Salt and pepper

1. Heat the oil in a skillet over medium-high. Add the onion and sauté until dark brown, about 30 to 60 minutes. Adjust the heat as necessary to keep the onions from scorching.

2. Simmer the tofu in enough water to cover for 10 minutes. Drain and transfer to a bowl. Cool, then mash.

3. Place the tofu, onion, green beans, and walnuts in a food processor, and purée into a smooth paste. Season with allspice, salt, and pepper. Chill thoroughly before serving.

Per ¼ cup: Calories 148, Protein 4 g, Carbohydrates 7 g, Fat 10 g

Spreads

Lentil and Walnut "Chopped Liver"

Makes 4 cups (about 12 servings)

A luscious mock liver pâté that is simply out of this world. Serve it on lettuce leaves or with crackers or rye bread. Your guests won't believe this isn't chopped liver!

1½ cups dry lentils
4 cups water
2 tablespoons extra-virgin olive oil
2 large onions, chopped
1 cup finely chopped or ground walnuts
1 tablespoon natural soy sauce (optional)
Salt and pepper

1. Rinse the lentils and place in a large saucepan with the water. Bring to a boil, reduce the heat, cover, and simmer for 45 minutes. Remove the cover and continue to simmer, stirring often, until any liquid has cooked off and the lentils are very tender.

2. Meanwhile, heat the oil in a large skillet. Add the onions and cook until very dark and caramelized, about 1 hour.

3. Place the lentils, onions, walnuts, soy sauce (if using), salt, and pepper in a food processor, and purée into a thick paste. Chill thoroughly before serving.

Per serving: Calories 150, Protein 5 g, Carbohydrates 14 g, Fat 8 g

Spreads

Cashew-Sesame Bean "Cheese"

Makes about 1 cup

The combination of cashew butter and tahini contributes a rich, sweet flavor reminiscent of dairy cream cheese. White beans round out the taste and minimize the fat.

½ cup drained cooked white beans
¼ cup fresh lemon juice
3 tablespoons cashew butter
2 tablespoons tahini
Salt
1 to 2 tablespoons water, if needed

Chop the beans in a food processor. Add the remaining ingredients, using the water only if needed to facilitate processing. Whip into a smooth, thick paste.

Per tablespoon: Calories 37, Protein 1 g, Carbohydrates 3 g, Fat 2 g

Tips:
• Cashew butter and tahini are available in natural food stores and some supermarkets. Raw (unroasted) butters will make the whitest, creamiest spreads. Pour off the oil that rises to the top. This will leave behind a thicker, drier butter which will make a firmer "cream cheese."

• Store opened jars of cashew butter and tahini in the refrigerator.

Spreads

Variations:

• For **Cashew-Sesame Bean "Cheese" with Chives or Scallions**, add 1 to 2 tablespoons finely chopped chives or scallions before or after processing.

• For **Cashew-Sesame Bean "Cheese" with Paprika**, add 1 teaspoon paprika with a pinch of cayenne pepper before processing.

• For **Cashew-Sesame Bean "Cheese" with Caraway and Pickles**, stir in 1 teaspoon ground caraway seeds, 2 teaspoons finely chopped pickles or well-drained pickle relish, and ground black pepper to taste before or after processing.

• For **Bean "Cheese" Gone Meshuga**, use all of the above variations at once.

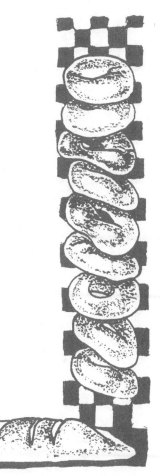

Spreads

White Bean "Salmon" Spread

Makes 1½ cups (2 to 4 servings)

Serve this attractive spread with toasted pita triangles and raw vegetables, or use it as a spread for bagels or bread.

1⅔ cups drained cooked white beans
2 tablespoons fresh lemon juice
1 tablespoon extra-virgin olive oil
¼ teaspoon crushed garlic
¼ teaspoon paprika
¼ cup minced fresh cilantro
Salt and pepper
Pinch of cayenne pepper

1. Chop the beans in a food processor. Add the lemon juice, olive oil, garlic, and paprika, and whip into a smooth paste.

2. Pulse in the cilantro and season with salt, pepper, and cayenne. Mix thoroughly. Serve at room temperature or chilled.

Per serving: Calories 182, Protein 8 g, Carbohydrates 26 g, Fat 5 g

Tip:
• If fresh cilantro is not available, use 1 teaspoon dried dill or tarragon.

Spreads

Tempeh "Tuna" Spread

Makes 3 to 4 servings

A healthful, high-protein spread that is both dolphin and tuna safe.

One 8-ounce package frozen tempeh, thawed and cut into
    cubes
1½ tablespoons cold water
⅓ cup Deli Dressing, p. 122, or vegan mayonnaise
2 tablespoons finely minced red onion
2 tablespoons finely diced celery
2 tablespoons minced fresh parsley
2 teaspoons prepared yellow mustard
2 teaspoons dried dill
Salt

1. Steam the tempeh for 20 minutes. Transfer to a bowl.
Immediately add the water and mash thoroughly using a fork
or potato masher.

2. Stir in the remaining ingredients and season with salt to
taste. Chill thoroughly before serving.

Per serving: Calories 183, Protein 13 g, Carbohydrates 13 g, Fat 8 g

Spreads

Hummus bi Tahini
(Chick-Pea and Tahini Dip)

Makes 4 to 6 servings

One of the finest recipes for this famous international dip. Pita bread is the traditional accompaniment, but raw vegetable crudités are great as well.

2 cups drained cooked chick-peas
½ cup water
1¼ teaspoons salt
¼ teaspoon crushed garlic
Pinch of cayenne pepper (optional)
½ cup fresh lemon juice
½ cup tahini
Paprika, as needed
Minced fresh parsley, or dried oregano (optional)

1. Blend or process the chick-peas with the water, salt, garlic, and cayenne pepper, if using, until smooth. Add the lemon juice and blend again. Gradually add the tahini and process until the mixture is thick and smooth.

2. To serve, spread the paste on a serving platter, and sprinkle with the paprika and parsley or oregano, if desired.

Per serving: Calories 251, Protein 9 g, Carbohydrates 26 g, Fat 11 g

Variations:
• Garnish with hot paprika or cayenne pepper instead of mild paprika.

• Add about 1 teaspoon ground cumin, or more to taste, during processing.

Spreads

Spiced Hummus

Makes about 2 cups

The best of the beloved bean dips!

1²/₃ cups drained cooked chick-peas
¼ cup tahini
3 tablespoons fresh lemon juice
1 tablespoon extra-virgin olive oil
1 tablespoon water, as needed
2 tablespoons chopped fresh parsley
½ teaspoon crushed garlic
¼ teaspoon ground cumin
¼ teaspoon ground coriander
¼ teaspoon paprika
Salt and cayenne pepper

Grind the beans in a food processor. Add the tahini, lemon juice, and oil, and blend into a coarse paste, adding about a tablespoon of water only if necessary to facilitate processing. The mixture should be very thick. Add the remaining ingredients and blend thoroughly.

Per ¼ cup: Calories 115, Protein 4 g, Carbohydrates 12 g, Fat 6 g

Spreads

White Bean Hummus

Makes 4 servings

Fresh herbs are the secret ingredient in this very special hummus.

2 cups drained cooked white beans
1 to 2 tablespoons fresh lemon juice
1½ tablespoons extra-virgin olive oil
1 tablespoon tahini
¾ teaspoon salt
½ teaspoon crushed garlic
Large pinch of cayenne pepper
¼ to ½ cup fresh basil or cilantro

Combine all the ingredients, except the fresh herbs, in a food processor, and blend into a smooth paste. Pulse in the herbs until they are coarsely chopped and evenly distributed.

Per serving: Calories 193, Protein 8 g, Carbohydrates 24 g, Fat 6 g

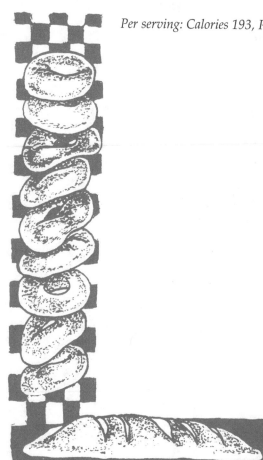

Spreads

Red Bean Hummus

Makes about 1½ cups

The splendid flavor of this dip is tantalizing and incomparable. It may soon become your favorite kind of hummus!

1⅔ cups drained cooked pinto beans
2 tablespoons tahini
1 tablespoon red wine vinegar
1 tablespoon natural soy sauce
¼ to ½ teaspoon bottled hot sauce
¼ teaspoon ground cumin
2 to 4 tablespoons sliced scallions

Combine the beans, tahini, vinegar, soy sauce, hot sauce, and cumin in a food processor, and blend into a smooth paste. Pulse in the scallions until finely chopped and evenly distributed.

Per ¼ cup: Calories 96, Protein 4 g, Carbohydrates 14 g, Fat 2 g

Spreads

Black Bean Hummus

Makes about 1½ cups

Dark, rich, mesmerizing black beans blend superbly with the rich tastes of balsamic vinegar and exotic spices.

1⅔ cups drained cooked black beans
2 tablespoons tahini
1 tablespoon natural soy sauce
1 tablespoon balsamic vinegar
¼ teaspoon crushed garlic
¼ teaspoon ground cumin
¼ teaspoon ground ginger
Large pinch of cayenne pepper

Combine all the ingredients in a food processor fitted with a metal blade, and blend into a smooth paste.

Per ¼ cup: Calories 93, Protein 5 g, Carbohydrates 13 g, Fat 2 g

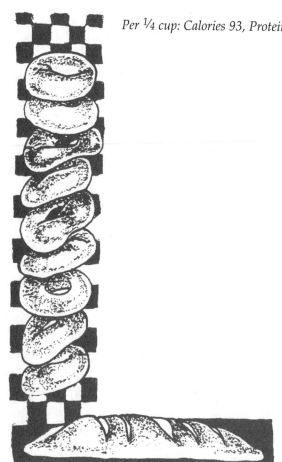

Spreads

Baba Ghanoush
(Eggplant and Tahini Purée)

Makes 6 servings

This classic eggplant dip entices everyone!

1 large eggplant
6 to 8 tablespoons tahini
1 tablespoon water
¼ cup fresh lemon juice
¼ teaspoon crushed garlic (optional)
Salt
Pepper or cayenne pepper (optional)
Finely chopped fresh parsley, dried oregano, or paprika

1. Prick the eggplant all over with a fork. Place on a dry baking sheet, and broil for about 45 minutes or until very soft when pressed and the skin is blistered and black. Cool.

2. Slit open and discard any large clusters of seeds. Scoop out the flesh into a colander; drain and gently press out the juices. Chop finely and transfer to a bowl. Mash well or, for a smoother consistency, purée in a blender or food processor.

3. Beat the tahini with the water. Then gradually add the lemon juice, and beat until smooth, creamy, and thick. Beat this mixture into the eggplant, then stir in the garlic (if using), salt, and pepper or cayenne, if desired. Chill thoroughly. To serve, spread on a platter and garnish with parsley, oregano, or paprika.

Per serving: Calories 127, Protein 3 g, Carbohydrates 11 g, Fat 7 g

Spreads

Mushroom-Pecan Pâté

Makes about 2 cups

This no-bake pâté has melt-in-your-mouth appeal. It's delicious as an appetizer mounded on lettuce leaves, as a spread for crackers, as a stuffing for celery sticks or mushroom caps, or as a sandwich filling.

½ pound firm regular tofu, rinsed
2 tablespoons extra-virgin olive oil
1 medium onion, chopped
½ cup pecans
2 cups chopped mushrooms
½ teaspoon dried thyme
1 tablespoon natural soy sauce
1 teaspoon salt
Pinch of pepper and ground nutmeg

1. Place the tofu in a saucepan with enough water to cover, and bring to a boil. Reduce the heat, cover, and simmer for 10 minutes. Drain and cool. Press gently to remove any excess water, and pat dry. Transfer to a bowl and mash.

2. Heat the oil in a large skillet. Add the onion and sauté over low heat until a deep golden brown, about 20 to 30 minutes. Add the pecans and continue to sauté for 10 minutes.

3. Add the mushrooms and thyme to the skillet, and cook, stirring often, for about 10 to 12 minutes longer or until the mushrooms are tender and nearly all of the liquid has cooked off.

4. Transfer the mixture to a food processor along with the tofu, soy sauce, salt, pepper, and nutmeg. Purée until very smooth and creamy. Chill thoroughly before serving.

Per 2 tablespoons: Calories 54, Protein 2 g, Carbohydrates 2 g, Fat 4 g

Spreads

Eggless Egg Salad

Makes about 2½ cups

A deli staple, this scrumptious salad is great in sandwiches, spread on crackers, stuffed into pita pockets, or scooped onto lettuce leaves. It's endlessly versatile any time of the day.

1 pound firm regular tofu, rinsed
½ cup Deli Dressing, p. 122, or vegan mayonnaise
½ cup diced celery
¼ cup minced fresh parsley (optional)
1 tablespoon finely minced onion or scallions
¼ teaspoon turmeric
Salt and pepper

1. Place the tofu in a saucepan with enough water to cover, and bring to a boil. Reduce the heat, cover, and simmer for 10 minutes. Drain and cool. Press gently to remove any excess water, and pat dry.

2. Transfer the tofu to a bowl and crumble finely. Add the remaining ingredients and season with salt and pepper to taste. Mix until well combined. Chill thoroughly before serving.

Per ½ cup: Calories 121, Protein 8 g, Carbohydrates 3 g, Fat 8 g

Spreads

Dressings

Dressings are what make deli salads taste special. A perfect dressing draws out delicate flavors without overpowering them. Dressings can also harmonize a hodgepodge of ingredients and help to create a unified blend of tastes. It's not necessary to have overly rich or complicated dressings; often a simple blend of oil and vinegar lends just the right touch to enliven a dish.

Here are a few basic dressings that can be made at the last minute. Many can be made in the quantity, consistency, and flavors you want, so they are suitable for any occasion.

Lemonade Dressing

This is an all-purpose dressing that's refreshing and light. Its delicate flavor can be made as sweet or sour as you like, making it ideal for vegetables, fruits, and combination salads. Because it's fat free, it's perfect for dishes with rich ingredients, such as nuts or avocado.

Fresh lemon juice
Liquid sweetener of your choice

Sweeten the lemon juice to taste, mixing thoroughly with a fork or mini-whisk.

Asian-Style Dressing

Toasted sesame oil adds exotic notes to this very simple dressing. It's great on vegetables and salads, but try it on fruit, too, and see what you think.

Brown rice vinegar
Toasted sesame oil
Natural soy sauce

Place a little of the vinegar in a small bowl. Add a few drops of sesame oil and soy sauce. Beat together with a fork or mini-whisk. Taste and add more vinegar, oil, or soy sauce as desired.

Dressings

Tossed Vinaigrette

This dressing is made directly in the bowl on top of the salad. It's the easiest way to dress a salad to suit your taste.

Extra-virgin olive oil
Wine vinegar
Fresh lemon juice
Salt and pepper
Optional seasonings (fresh or dried herbs or garlic)

Sprinkle a little oil over the salad. Start with 1 or 2 table-spoons depending on the size of the salad. Toss until every-thing is very lightly coated. Sprinkle on the vinegar and a lit-tle lemon juice, a pinch of salt, and freshly ground pepper. If you like, add a light shower of fresh or dried herbs and crushed garlic. Toss well so everything is evenly distributed. If done properly, there should be no puddle of dressing in the bottom of the bowl.

Mustard Dressing

Toss this delightful mixture with salads, or use as a sauce or dip for vegetables, or as a dressing for potato salad.

Dijon mustard
Liquid sweetener of your choice
Extra-virgin olive oil or canola oil

Sweeten the mustard to taste. Then add a little oil to soften the flavor.

Dressings

Nut or Seed Butter Dressing

When nut or seed butter is used instead of oil, a whole new realm of possibilities emerges. There are so many butters to choose from; use one or a combination. All measurements are approximations, as this recipe begs for your own creative touch.

1/2 cup nut or seed butter
1/4 to 1/2 cup water
1/4 cup vinegar or fresh lemon juice
Salt or natural soy sauce
Black or red pepper
Additional seasonings (herbs, garlic, ginger, wet or dry
    mustard, toasted sesame oil, sweetener)

1. Thin the butter with the water, beating in just a small amount at a time

2. Gradually beat in the vinegar or lemon juice to taste, starting with just a teaspoonful or two.

3. Add salt, pepper, and any seasonings you desire. Sweetener is optional, but a little will counterbalance too much tartness. If the dressing is too thick, add a little water. If it is too thin, add more nut or seed butter. Keep in mind that the dressing will thicken a bit when chilled. Store leftover dressing in the refrigerator.

Per tablespoon: Calories 48, Protein 2 g, Carbohydrates 2 g, Fat 4 g

Deli Dressing

Makes about 1½ cups

This is the perfect, low-fat substitute for traditional egg-laden mayonnaise. It's rich tasting without being high in fat and creamy without containing any eggs or dairy products.

1½ cups mashed firm silken tofu
3 tablespoons fresh lemon juice
½ teaspoon salt
¼ teaspoon dry mustard
¼ cup canola oil

Place the tofu, lemon juice, salt, and dry mustard in a blender or food processor, and process until smooth and creamy. With the appliance running, drizzle in the oil in a slow, steady stream through the cap opening in the lid. Store in the refrigerator. It will keep for at least a week.

Per 2 tablespoons: Calories 64, Protein 3 g, Carbohydrates 1 g, Fat 5 g

Dressings

Sour Dressing

Makes about 1½ cups

Use this delicious, creamy topping wherever you would use dairy sour cream. It's low in fat, cholesterol-free, and contains no gums or gelatin, which are typically found in the "real" thing.

1½ cups mashed firm silken tofu
2 tablespoons fresh lemon juice
1 tablespoon white wine vinegar
½ teaspoon salt
⅛ teaspoon ground coriander
2 tablespoons canola oil

1. Place the tofu, lemon juice, vinegar, salt, and coriander in a blender or food processor, and process until smooth and creamy.

2. With the appliance running, drizzle in the oil in a slow steady stream through the cap opening in the lid. Store in the refrigerator. It will keep for at least a week.

Per 2 tablespoons: Calories 43, Protein 3 g, Carbohydrates 1 g, Fat 3 g

"Cream Cheese" Sauce

Makes about 1¼ cups

Silken tofu becomes extra thick and sumptuous with the addition of rich, creamy cashew butter. It tastes like a combination of cream cheese, sour cream, and yogurt all in one, and can be used with equal versatility.

1 cup mashed firm silken tofu
1 to 2 tablespoons cashew butter
Fresh lemon juice
Salt
Soymilk (optional)

Blend the tofu with the cashew butter. Add lemon juice to taste, along with a tiny pinch of salt. If the mixture becomes too thick, thin it with a little soymilk.

Per 2 tablespoons: Calories 34, Protein 3 g, Carbohydrates 2 g, Fat 1 g

Dressings

Tahina

Makes about 1 cup

This luscious, creamy sauce is served as a dip or dressing. Use it sparingly, as it is very rich.

½ cup tahini
1 teaspoon salt
¼ teaspoon crushed garlic
Pinch of cayenne pepper (optional)
½ cup water
½ cup fresh lemon juice
Paprika (optional)
Minced fresh parsley (optional)

1. Combine the tahini, salt, garlic, and cayenne, if using, in a bowl, and mix well using a fork.

2. Very gradually beat in the water, and continue beating with the fork for about one minute. Very gradually beat in the lemon juice, and blend well. At first the sauce will turn white and seize up, but keep beating. It will eventually thin out and become smooth and creamy.

3. To use as a dip, spread on a platter and garnish with paprika and parsley. To use as a dressing, thin with a little more water.

Per tablespoon: Calories 45, Protein 1 g, Carbohydrates 3 g, Fat 2 g

Dressings

Soups

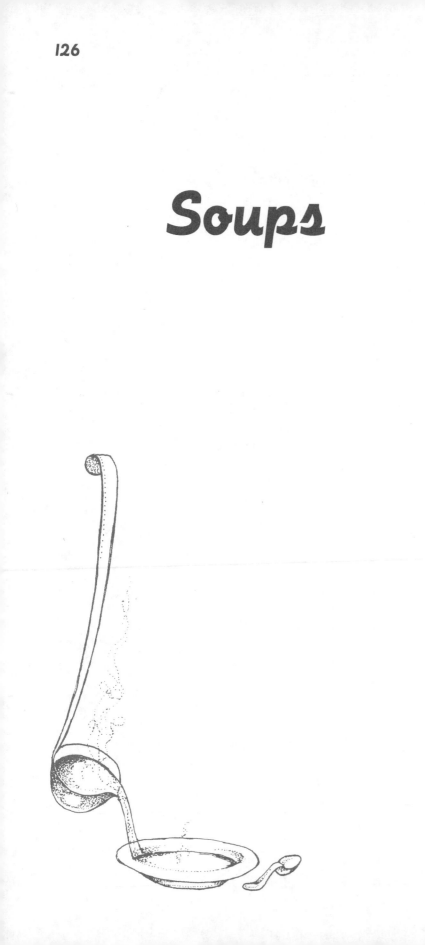

Sauerkraut Soup

Makes 1½ quarts

This Eastern European specialty is delicious as an appetizer or a light supper. Serve it with thick slices of a hearty pumpernickel or herb bread.

4 cups water
2 cups drained sauerkraut
1½ cups chopped onions
¼ cup tomato paste
2 tablespoons sugar
2 teaspoons sweet paprika
1 teaspoon caraway seeds
Sour Dressing, p 123, to pass at the table (optional)

Combine the water, sauerkraut, onions, tomato paste, sugar, paprika, and caraway seeds in a large soup pot, and bring to a boil. Reduce the heat to low, cover, and simmer for 30 minutes. Serve hot, with Sour Dressing on the side, if desired.

Per cup: Calories 52, Protein 1 g, Carbohydrates 12 g, Fat 0 g

I added Old World Seasoning (Penzeys)

salt

Soups

Better Than Chicken Noodle Soup

Makes 6 servings

The name says it all!

10 cups water
2 carrots, cut into large chunks
1 large onion, quartered
1 leek, sliced
1 turnip, quartered
2 stalks celery, with leaves, cut into large slices
4 sprigs of parsley
1 teaspoon whole black peppercorns
2 bay leaves
4 carrots, cut in half lengthwise, then sliced widthwise into
    large pieces
A handful of minced fresh parsley
1 tablespoon extra-virgin olive oil
Salt and white pepper
Handful of fine noodles

1. Combine the water, carrot chunks, onion, leek, turnip, celery, parsley sprigs, peppercorns, and bay leaves in a large soup pot, and bring to a boil. Reduce the heat, cover, and simmer for 1 hour.

Soups

2. Strain the broth and return it to the pot. Add the sliced carrot pieces and minced parsley, and bring to a boil. Reduce the heat, cover, and simmer until the carrots are tender, about 20 to 30 minutes. Season with olive oil, salt, and white pepper.

3. A few minutes before serving, add a handful of fine noodles, broken into pieces in your hand, and simmer until tender. Serve very hot.

Per serving: Calories 111, Protein 2 g, Carbohydrates 20 g, Fat 2 g

Variation:
• For **Better Than Chicken Rice Soup**, substitute 1 to 1½ cups cooked rice for the fine noodles.

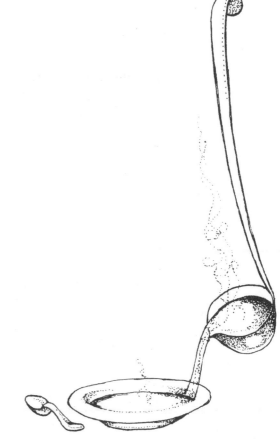

Soups

Goulash

Makes 4 to 6 servings

Use a little less water to make a stew or a little more to make a thin soup.

2 tablespoons extra-virgin olive oil
1 large onion, chopped
1½ pounds potatoes (about 5 to 6 medium), cubed or
    quartered
2 cups drained cooked kidney beans
2 fresh tomatoes, peeled and chopped
1 green or red bell pepper, diced
1 tablespoon sweet paprika
8 cups water

Heat the oil in a large soup pot. Add the onion and sauté until golden. Stir in the potatoes, beans, tomatoes, bell pepper, and paprika, and mix well. Stir in the water and bring to a boil. Simmer, stirring occasionally, for about 1 hour.

Per serving: Calories 278, Protein 8 g, Carbohydrates 49 g, Fat 6 g

Variations:
• If desired, sauté ½ teaspoon crushed garlic along with the onion. Sauerkraut, cabbage, and/or pasta may also be added.

Soups

Mushroom and Barley Soup

Makes 8 servings

Taste the rich, earthy flavors of the Old World in every spoonful of this classic soup.

8 ounces fresh mushrooms
2 medium potatoes
2 small onions
2 small carrots
2 celery stalks with leaves
10 cups water
⅓ cup pearl barley
Salt and pepper
Sour Dressing, p. 123, to pass at the table (optional)

1. Chop all the vegetables very finely. (A food processor will work best.)

2. Combine the vegetables in a large soup pot with the water and barley. Bring to a boil, reduce the heat, cover, and simmer, stirring occasionally, for 1 hour, or until the barley is very soft and swelled. Season with plenty of salt and pepper. Serve hot with Sour Dressing on the side, if desired.

Per serving: Calories 81, Protein 2 g, Carbohydrates 18 g, Fat 0 g

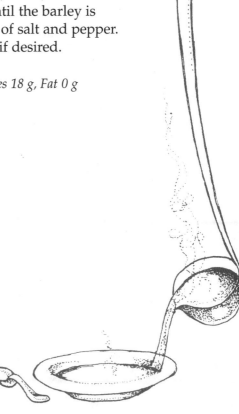

Soups

Mushroom and Potato Soup

Makes 6 servings

This moderately chunky soup is warming, filling, and easy to prepare.

1 pound potatoes (about 2 large or 3 to 4 medium), peeled
    and chopped
6 cups water
8 ounces fresh mushrooms
3 tablespoons extra-virgin olive oil
Salt and pepper
¼ cup minced fresh parsley
Lemon wedges
Sour Dressing, p. 123, to pass at the table (optional)

1. Place the potatoes and water in a large soup pot, and bring to a boil. Reduce the heat, cover, and simmer until very soft and starting to fall apart. Mash the potatoes in the pot with a potato masher.

2. Finely mince the mushrooms with a knife or in a food processor, and sauté them in the oil for 5 minutes. Add to the pot with the potatoes, season with salt and pepper, and simmer for a few minutes. Stir in the parsley just before serving. Serve accompanied with lemon wedges and Sour Dressing on the side, if desired.

Per serving: Calories 136, Protein 1 g, Carbohydrates 17 g, Fat 7 g

Soups

Leek and Potato Soup

Makes 6 servings

Potatoes and onions are a heavenly pair. This scrumptious soup uses a combination of healthful leeks and delicate chives or scallions for a complex blend of onion flavors.

1 pound potatoes (about 2 large or 3 to 4 medium)
1 pound leeks
4½ cups water
2 cups plain soymilk
Salt and white pepper
1 cup Sour Dressing, p. 123
¼ cup minced scallions or chives

1. Peel and cube the potatoes. Trim the leeks and mince them finely. Place the potatoes and leeks in a large soup pot with the water, soymilk, salt, and pepper. Simmer gently for 1 hour, stirring often.

2. Mash the potatoes in the pot with a potato masher. Stir in the Sour Dressing. Serve the soup hot or thoroughly chilled, garnished with the scallions or chives.

Per serving: Calories 195, Protein 7 g, Carbohydrates 29 g, Fat 5 g

Tip:
• Soymilk is recommended because it has less tendency to curdle at high heat than other nondairy milks.

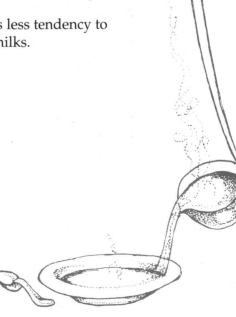

Soups

Green Potato Soup

Makes 6 servings

This beautiful green soup is astonishingly simple, delicious, and healthful.

2 tablespoons extra-virgin olive oil
1 large onion, coarsely chopped
1 teaspoon crushed garlic
6 cups water
4 large potatoes, peeled and chopped
Salt and pepper
1 large bunch fresh parsley, washed, stems removed
1 to 1½ cups plain soymilk, as needed

1. Heat the oil in a large soup pot. Add the onion and sauté until tender. Add the garlic and sauté for 1 minute. Stir in the water, potatoes, salt, and pepper, and bring to a boil. Reduce the heat, cover, and simmer until the potatoes are tender and starting to fall apart, about 45 minutes.

2. Remove from the heat and purée in batches in a blender along with the parsley. Return to the pot and add enough milk to thin to your liking. Heat through, stirring often, but do not boil. Serve hot.

Per serving: Calories 144, Protein 3 g, Carbohydrates 21 g, Fat 5 g

Lentil and Rice Soup

Makes 6 to 8 servings

Simple ingredients blend to make a hearty lentil soup that is out of this world.

8 cups water
1 cup dried lentils, rinsed and drained
½ cup brown rice, rinsed and drained
1 large onion, chopped
¼ cup extra-virgin olive oil
Salt and pepper

1. Combine the water, lentils, and rice in a large soup pot, and bring to a boil. Reduce the heat, cover, and simmer 1½ to 2 hours, stirring occasionally, until the lentils are very tender and the soup is thick. Add a little extra water during cooking, if necessary.

2. Meanwhile, sauté the onion in the olive oil over very low heat for 30 to 60 minutes or until very tender and dark brown. Add the onion and oil to the soup, season with salt and pepper, and simmer 10 to 15 minutes longer.

Per serving: Calories 199, Protein 7 g, Carbohydrates 25 g, Fat 8 g

Soups

Thick Lentil Purée

Makes 4 to 6 servings

A smooth, energizing, high-protein soup, so thick you could almost eat it with a fork — but do use a spoon so you won't miss a single drop.

2 tablespoons extra-virgin olive oil
1 large onion, diced
2 celery stalks, diced
1 teaspoon crushed garlic
2 cups dried lentils, rinsed and drained
8 cups water
2 bay leaves
¼ cup fresh lemon juice
1 to 2 teaspoons ground cumin
Salt and pepper
Minced fresh parsley for garnish

1. Heat the oil in a large soup pot. Add the onion and sauté until it starts to brown. Add the celery and garlic, and sauté for 5 minutes. Add the lentils, water, and bay leaf, and bring to a boil. Reduce the heat, cover, and cook for 1 hour. Season with the lemon juice, cumin, salt, and pepper, and simmer 10 minutes longer. Remove the bay leaves.

2. Purée ⅓ to ½ of the soup in batches in a blender. Return to the pot with the remaining soup, and heat through. If the soup seems too thin, simmer until slightly thickened, making sure it doesn't stick or burn on the bottom of the pot. Serve hot, garnished with parsley.

Per serving: Calories 271, Protein 14 g, Carbohydrates 40 g, Fat 6 g

Soups

Red Lentil Soup

Makes 6 servings

A quick, low-fat, staple recipe with lots of variation possibilities to keep it fresh and different every time you make it.

7 cups water
2½ cups dried red lentils, rinsed and drained
1 large onion, minced
2 to 4 tablespoons fresh lemon juice
1 teaspoon ground cumin
Salt and pepper

1. Combine the water, lentils, and onion in a large soup pot, and bring to a boil. Reduce the heat, partially cover, and simmer until the lentils have disintegrated, about 30 to 60 minutes.

2. Stir in the lemon juice, cumin, salt, and pepper, and serve hot.

Per serving: Calories 203, Protein 13 g, Carbohydrates 36 g, Fat 0 g

Variations:
• Finely chop an additional large onion, and sauté it in 3 tablespoons olive oil over very low heat until very dark brown and caramelized, about 30 to 60 minutes. Add to the soup at the end.

• Omit the cumin. Sauté 1 teaspoon crushed garlic in 3 tablespoons olive oil for 1 minute. Add to the soup at the end along with 2 teaspoons dried spearmint.

• Add 1 teaspoon turmeric and a large pinch of cayenne pepper at the beginning.

• Add 2 peeled and chopped ripe tomatoes shortly before the soup has finished cooking.

Soups

Lemony Lentil Soup
with Noodles and Mint

Makes 6 to 8 servings

A refreshingly different lentil soup with a burst of bright flavor in every bite.

7 cups water
2½ cups dried red lentils, rinsed and drained
3 tablespoons extra-virgin olive oil
2 large onions, minced
1 teaspoon crushed garlic
¼ cup fresh lemon juice
1 tablespoon dried spearmint
Salt and pepper
5 ounces thin noodles, broken into small pieces

1. Combine the water and lentils in a large soup pot, and bring to a boil. Reduce the heat, partially cover, and simmer until the lentils have disintegrated, about 30 to 60 minutes.

2. Heat the oil in a large skillet, and sauté the onion until dark brown. Stir in the garlic and sauté for 1 minute. Add to the soup along with the lemon juice, spearmint, salt, and pepper. About 10 minutes before serving, stir the noodles into the soup.

Per serving: Calories 263, Protein 13 g, Carbohydrates 39 g, Fat 6 g

Soups

Green Split Pea Soup

Makes about 1½ quarts

Hearty and satisfying. Like most bean soups, it's even better the next day when the flavors have mingled overnight.

2 tablespoons extra-virgin olive oil
1 large onion, chopped
1 cup chopped carrots
½ teaspoon crushed garlic
6 cups water
1½ cups dried green split peas, soaked overnight
Salt and pepper

1. Heat the oil in a large soup pot, and sauté the onion, carrots, and garlic until soft. Drain the peas, rinse well, and add to the pot along with the water. Bring to a boil, reduce the heat, cover, and simmer, stirring occasionally, until the peas have practically disintegrated, about 1½ to 2 hours.

2. Season with salt and pepper. Serve as is or blend for a smoother texture.

Per cup: Calories 250, Protein 12 g, Carbohydrates 37 g, Fat 6 g

Tip:
• If leftover soup becomes too thick, thin it with a little extra water or serve like a stew over rice or bulgur.

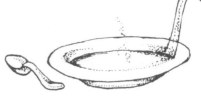

Soups

Yellow Split Pea Soup
with "Frankfurters"

Makes 8 to 10 servings

A rich and appetizing soup.

3 tablespoons extra-virgin olive oil
1 large onion, chopped
2 carrots, sliced
2 cups yellow split peas, soaked overnight
8 cups water
2 bay leaves
Salt and pepper
8 vegetarian "hot dogs," sliced
2 to 4 tablespoons fresh lemon juice

1. Heat the oil in a large soup pot, and sauté the onion and carrots until soft. Drain the peas, rinse well, and add to the pot along with the water. Bring to a boil, reduce the heat, cover, and simmer, stirring occasionally, until the peas have practically disintegrated, about $1\frac{1}{2}$ to 2 hours.

2. Purée the soup in batches in a blender, and return to the pot. Add the bay leaves, salt, and pepper. Thin with additional water if the soup is too thick, and simmer for 30 minutes longer. Remove the bay leaves. Add the sliced "hot dogs" and lemon juice, and cook a few minutes more. Serve hot.

Per serving: Calories 245, Protein 15 g, Carbohydrates 30 g, Fat 7 g

Spicy Italian Chick-Pea Soup

Makes 6 servings

Bean soup with a delightful kick!

2 tablespoons extra-virgin olive oil
1 large onion, chopped
1 teaspoon crushed garlic
6 cups drained cooked chick-peas
6 cups water
4 or 5 peeled fresh or canned tomatoes, chopped
4 tablespoons tomato paste
1/2 teaspoon dried thyme
1/2 teaspoon dried oregano
Salt and pepper
Pinch of cayenne pepper
Minced fresh parsley for garnish (optional)

1. Heat the olive oil in a large soup pot. Add the onion and sauté until tender. Add the garlic and sauté for 1 minute.

2. Stir in the chick-peas, water, tomatoes, tomato paste, and seasonings. Bring to a boil, reduce the heat, cover, and simmer for 40 minutes, stirring occasionally. Serve hot, garnished with parsley, if desired.

Per serving: Calories 344, Protein 14 g, Carbohydrates 53 g, Fat 7 g

Soups

Moroccan Chick-Pea Soup

Makes 6 servings

Spicy and flavorful, this soup is similar to an Indian curry.

6 cups water
3 cups drained cooked chick-peas
1 large potato, peeled and diced
½ cup minced onion
4 tablespoons tomato paste
1 teaspoon ground cumin
½ teaspoon ground ginger
¼ teaspoon turmeric
Salt and cayenne pepper
½ cup minced fresh cilantro or parsley

1. Combine all the ingredients, except the cilantro or parsley, in a large soup pot, and bring to a boil. Reduce the heat, cover, and simmer for 1 hour.

2. Remove 2 cups of the soup, and purée in a blender. Return to the pot and mix well. Stir in the cilantro or parsley just before serving.

Per serving: Calories 169, Protein 7 g, Carbohydrates 30 g, Fat 1 g

Soups

White Bean and Cabbage Soup

Makes 6 servings

A mild, naturally sweet bean soup laced with bobbing flecks of winter squash.

2 tablespoons extra-virgin olive oil
1 large onion, chopped
1 teaspoon crushed garlic
8 cups water
3 cups drained cooked white beans
1 small head green cabbage, finely chopped
½ pound winter squash or pumpkin, peeled and chopped
    (about 1½ cups)
1 teaspoon dried thyme
Salt and pepper

1. Heat the oil in a large soup pot. Add the onion and sauté until it begins to brown. Add the garlic and sauté for 1 minute. Add the remaining ingredients and bring to a boil.

2. Reduce the heat, cover, and simmer, stirring occasionally, for 1 hour.

Per serving: Calories 202, Protein 8 g, Carbohydrates 31 g, Fat 5 g

Soups

White Bean and Black Olive Soup

Makes about 1½ quarts (4 to 6 servings)

This recipe combines both gentle and robust tastes to make an outstanding and memorable bowl of soup.

4 cups water
1½ cups drained cooked white beans
4 stalks celery, with leaves, chopped
2 medium potatoes, peeled and diced
2 tablespoons tomato paste
½ teaspoon salt
⅛ teaspoon pepper
¼ cup sliced black olives

1. Combine the water, beans, celery, potatoes, tomato paste, salt, and pepper in a large soup pot, and bring to a boil. Reduce the heat, cover, and simmer for 40 minutes.

2. Stir in the olives. Serve hot.

Per serving: Calories 144, Protein 6 g, Carbohydrates 27 g, Fat 1 g

Soups

Classic Onion Soup

Makes about 1½ quarts (4 servings)

A time-honored favorite that's amazingly simple to prepare.

1 tablespoon extra-virgin olive oil
2 large onions, cut in half and thinly sliced
1 tablespoon crushed garlic
¼ cup flour (whole wheat, barley, rye, or spelt)
4 cups water
¼ cup natural soy sauce
Toasted whole grain bread cubes (about ¼ cup per serving)

1. Heat the oil in a large soup pot. Add the onions and garlic, and sauté for 5 minutes. Stir in the flour, mixing well. Then stir in the water and soy sauce, and bring to a boil. Reduce the heat, cover, and simmer until the onions are tender, about 20 minutes.

2. Just before serving, place bread cubes in the bottom of each soup bowl. Ladle the soup on top, and serve.

Per serving: Calories 118, Protein 4 g, Carbohydrates 16 g, Fat 5 g

Soups

Creamy Carrot Bisque
with Exotic Spices

Makes 6 to 8 servings

Although there are no dairy products in this exotically flavored soup, the texture is very creamy.

2 tablespoons extra-virgin olive oil
1 large onion, coarsely chopped
1 pound carrots, trimmed, scraped, and sliced
1 large potato, peeled and coarsely chopped
½ teaspoon ground cardamom
½ teaspoon ground cinnamon
¼ teaspoon ground ginger
¼ teaspoon ground nutmeg
Salt and cayenne pepper
6 to 8 cups hot vegetable stock or water

1. Heat the olive oil in a large soup pot or Dutch oven. Add the onion and sauté for 5 minutes. Stir in the carrots and potato, and stir until coated with the oil. Add the nutmeg, cardamom, cinnamon, salt, and cayenne, and sauté for 10 minutes.

2. Pour in the hot stock or water, and bring to a boil. Reduce the heat, cover, and simmer until the vegetables are very tender, about 30 minutes. Purée in batches in a blender. Serve hot.

Per serving: Calories 86, Protein 1 g, Carbohydrates 12 g, Fat 4 g

Soups

Squash Soup

Makes 8 servings

A light but satisfying soup. The Sour Dressing is optional, but it will add a delicious sour flavor that counterbalances the soup's delicate sweetness.

3½ pounds winter squash
2 pounds potatoes (about 4 large or 6 to 8 medium), peeled
    and cubed
10 cups plain soymilk
Salt and white pepper
2 tablespoons sugar
1 cup Sour Dressing, p. 123, to pass at the table (optional)

1. Peel the squash, scrape away the seeds and fibers, and cut into cubes. Place in a large soup pot with the potatoes, soymilk, salt, pepper, and sugar. Bring to a boil, reduce the heat to low, cover, and simmer until the squash and potatoes are very soft, about 30 minutes.

2. Mash the vegetables in the pot with a potato masher. Adjust the seasonings, if necessary, and simmer a few minutes longer. Serve hot, accompanied with Sour Dressing on the side, if desired.

Per serving: Calories 284, Protein 10 g, Carbohydrates 47 g, Fat 6 g

Tip:
• Soymilk is recommended because it has less tendency to curdle at high heat than other nondairy milks.

Soups

Borscht
(Cold Beet Soup)

Makes 4 to 6 servings

Beets were well utilized in the "old country," and borscht was among the favored ways to prepare them.

1 pound fresh beets (three to four 2-inch beets) with greens, if
     available
8 cups water
Salt and pepper
2 to 4 tablespoons fresh lemon juice
1 to 2 tablespoons sugar
4 to 6 peeled and boiled potatoes (optional)
1 cup Sour Dressing, p. 123, to pass at the table

1. Trim the beets and scrub them well. Wash and chop the greens, if available, and set aside.

2. Bring the water and beets to a boil in a large soup pot. Reduce the heat, cover, and simmer until the beets are fork tender, about 40 minutes.

3. Remove the beets with a slotted spoon, and let cool. Peel (using your hands), dice, and return to the cooking water.

4. Add the greens and a pinch of salt and pepper, and simmer for 15 minutes. Add the lemon juice and sugar, and chill thoroughly. Serve with boiled potatoes, if desired, and Sour Dressing on the side.

Per serving: Calories 121, Protein 5 g, Carbohydrates 12 g, Fat 6 g

Tips:
• If beet greens are not available, they may be omitted.

• Serving the soup with hot boiled potatoes makes a pleasant contrast in textures and temperatures.

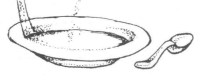

Soups

Fruit Soup

Makes 6 servings

An old tradition in Eastern Europe — especially Poland, Hungary, and Germany — was to serve stewed fruit as a starter to sharpen the appetite. It can be served hot, but is most commonly chilled.

5 pounds mixed fresh fruit, peeled and chopped (choose from
    apples, plums, apricots, peaches, pears, nectarines,
    berries, or rhubarb)
3 cups water
4 to 6 tablespoons fresh lemon juice
2 to 5 tablespoons sugar
Flavoring options: cinnamon, lemon peel, and/or vanilla
Boiled potatoes (optional)
Sour Dressing, p. 123 (optional)

1. Combine the fruit, water, lemon juice, sugar, and flavoring options in a large soup pot, and bring to a boil. Reduce the heat, cover, and simmer until soft, about 15 minutes.

2. Keep chunky by mashing with a potato masher, or blend to a light purée. Serve hot with potatoes or cold with Sour Dressing, if desired.

Per serving: Calories 168, Protein 2 g, Carbohydrates 38 g, Fat 0 g

Soups

Hot Specialties
(Noodles, Grains & Vegetables)

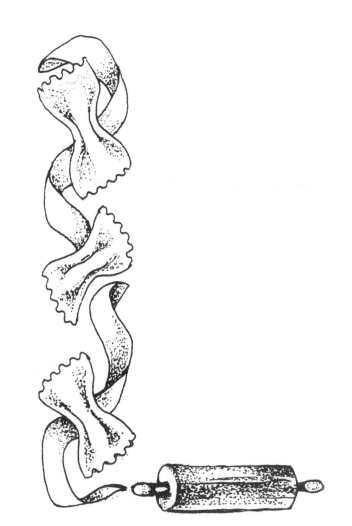

Lokshen Kugel
(Savory Noodle Pudding)

Makes 6 to 8 servings

The Yiddish word for noodles, "lokshen," was derived from the Polish word "lokszyn." Homemade lokshen were once a staple part of the Sabbath meals for Jews, although today hardly anyone makes them at home because noodles are so readily available. Lokshen kugel is either savory or sweet. This one is a simple savory version.

12 ounces egg-free wide noodles
1 large onion, chopped
3 tablespoons canola oil
1½ cups Sour Dressing, p. 123
Salt

1. Boil the noodles in salted water until just tender. Drain well and transfer to a large bowl.

2. Sauté the onion in the oil over low heat until browned, about 20 to 30 minutes or longer. Add to the noodles along with the Sour Dressing and a little salt to taste. Mix well.

3. Preheat the oven to 350°F. Oil a 4-quart casserole dish that is large enough to hold the noodle mixture. A deep casserole will make a moister kugel; a shallow casserole will make a crispier kugel. Pour the mixture into the prepared casserole, and bake uncovered until firm and lightly brown on top, about 30 minutes. Cut into squares and serve hot.

Per serving: Calories 205, Protein 7 g, Carbohydrates 18 g, Fat 12 g

Variation:
• For **Sweet and Peppery Lokshen Kugel**, add ½ cup sugar, ½ cup raisins, and 1½ teaspoons ground black pepper.

Hot Specialties

Lokshen Kugel with Apple
(Noodle Pudding with Apple)

Makes 6 to 8 servings

This traditional sweet pudding has been made by Jews in Germany since the Middle Ages. It makes an excellent hot or cold side dish, breakfast, or dessert.

12 ounces egg-free wide noodles
1 cup Sour Dressing, p. 123
¾ cup sugar
¾ cup coarsely chopped walnuts
¾ cup currants or raisins
Zest of 1 lemon or orange
4 tart apples (such as Granny Smith)
2 tablespoons fresh lemon juice

1. Boil the noodles in lightly salted water until tender; drain.

2. Combine the Sour Dressing and sugar in a large bowl. Stir in the walnuts, currants or raisins, and lemon or orange zest. Stir in the drained noodles.

Hot Specialties

3. Preheat the oven to 350° F. Peel, core, and coarsely grate or finely chop the apples. Toss them with the lemon juice, then add them to the noodle mixture and mix well.

4. Oil a 5-quart casserole dish that is large enough to hold the noodle mixture, and spoon the mixture into it. A deep casserole will make a moister kugel; a shallow casserole will make a crispier kugel. Cover with a lid or foil, and bake until firm and lightly browned, about 50 minutes.

Per serving: Calories 373, Protein 8 g, Carbohydrates 60 g, Fat 11 g

Variation:
• Omit the lemon or orange zest, and season with 2 teaspoons ground cinnamon, ¼ teaspoon ground nutmeg, and a pinch of ground cloves.

Hot Specialties

Lokshen Kugel with "Cheese"
(Creamy Noodle Pudding)

Makes 6 to 8 servings

Creamy noodle kugel is the most sumptuous version of this magnificent dish.

12 ounces egg-free wide noodles
1 tablespoon canola oil
2½ cups Sour Dressing, p. 123
½ pound firm regular tofu, mashed
Salt
Good pinch of nutmeg (optional)

1. Boil the noodles in salted water until just tender; drain well. Transfer to a large bowl, and toss with the oil.

2. Combine the remaining ingredients in a separate bowl, and season with salt and nutmeg. Add to the cooked noodles, and mix well.

3. Preheat the oven to 350°F. Oil a 4-quart casserole dish that is large enough to hold the noodle mixture. A deep casserole will make a moister kugel; a shallow casserole will make a crispier kugel. Pour the mixture into the prepared casserole, and bake uncovered until firm and lightly brown on top, about 30 minutes. Serve hot or cold cut into squares.

Per serving: Calories 231, Protein 12 g, Carbohydrates 19 g, Fat 12 g

Variation:
• For a sweet dessert kugel, omit the nutmeg. Add ½ cup sugar, the grated zest of an orange or a lemon, and ½ cup golden or black raisins or dried cherries.

Hot Specialties

Potato Kugel
(Grated Potato Pudding)

Makes 6 servings

Potato kugel makes a scrumptious side dish or satisfying entrée. It is perfect for share-a-dish gatherings and is a welcome companion to any cold deli salad.

6 medium potatoes, peeled and grated
1 large onion, grated
⅓ cup whole wheat flour
1 teaspoon salt
Pinch of nutmeg, pepper, and cayenne pepper

1. Preheat the oven to 350°F. Combine the onion and potatoes in a large bowl. Sprinkle the remaining ingredients on top, and mix thoroughly, using your hands, if necessary, to distribute the flour and seasonings evenly.

2. Oil a 4-quart casserole large enough to hold the potato mixture. A small, deep casserole will make a softer, more moist kugel; a wide, shallow casserole will result in more of a brown, crispy crust. Spoon in the mixture, smooth out the top, and bake until firm and golden brown, about 1 hour. Serve hot or at room temperature.

Per serving: Calories 147, Protein 3 g, Carbohydrates 34 g, Fat 0 g

Variation:
• For **Potato Kugel with Cabbage**, mix in ¾ pound of cabbage, cut into thin ribbons, and steamed or boiled in salted water just until tender.

Tip:
• For ease of preparation, grate the potatoes and onion in a food processor fitted with a shredding blade.

Hot Specialties

Scrambled Tofu and Onion

Makes 4 servings

This simple Polish dish is traditionally made with eggs. Tofu makes an excellent and soothing replacement.

3 tablespoons extra-virgin olive oil
1 large onion, coarsely chopped
1 pound tofu, rinsed, patted dry, and crumbled
Large pinch of turmeric
Salt and pepper
2 to 4 tablespoons finely chopped chives or scallions

1. Heat the oil in a large skillet. Add the onion and sauté until soft and golden brown.

2. Add the tofu, turmeric, salt, pepper, and chives or scallions. Stir-fry with a metal spatula until very hot and starting to brown, about 10 minutes.

Per serving: Calories 197, Protein 9 g, Carbohydrates 5 g, Fat 14 g

Kasha Varnishkes
(Buckwheat Groats and Pasta)

Makes 4 servings

A famous Jewish dish.

2 tablespoons canola or olive oil
1 medium onion, julienned
6 ounces bow-tie noodles
2 cups lightly salted water
1 cup roasted buckwheat groats
Salt and pepper

1. Heat the oil in a large skillet. Add the onion and sauté over low heat until very tender and browned, about 30 to 60 minutes.

2. Cook the pasta until tender. Drain and set aside.

3. Bring the water to a boil in a medium saucepan. Add the buckwheat and stir. Reduce the heat to low, cover, and simmer until the grain is tender and the water is absorbed, about 15 minutes.

4. Combine the browned onions with the pasta and cooked buckwheat. Season with salt and pepper. Serve hot.

Per serving: Calories 217, Protein 4 g, Carbohydrates 33 g, Fat 7 g

Hot Specialties

Kasha with Mushrooms
(Buckwheat Groats and Mushrooms)

Makes 4 servings

A traditional deli standard.

2 tablespoons canola or olive oil
1 large onion, julienned
½ pound mushrooms, sliced or quartered
2 cups lightly salted water
1 cup roasted buckwheat groats
Salt and pepper

1. Heat the oil in a large skillet. Add the onion and sauté over low heat until very tender and browned, about 30 to 60 minutes. Add the mushrooms and cook, stirring often, until tender.

2. Bring the water to a boil in a medium saucepan. Add the buckwheat and stir. Reduce the heat to low, cover, and simmer until the grain is tender and the water is absorbed, about 15 minutes.

3. Combine the onions and mushrooms with the cooked buckwheat, and season with salt and pepper. Heat through if necessary. Serve hot.

Per serving: Calories 186, Protein 3 g, Carbohydrates 25 g, Fat 7 g

Hot Specialties

Barley

Makes 3 to 4 servings.

Barley was the primary staple in Eastern Europe, before the potato gained dominion in the nineteenth century. It's still a popular side dish.

3 cups water
1 cup pearl barley
1 teaspoon salt
2 tablespoons canola or extra-virgin olive oil or Sour
    Dressing, p. 123

1. Place the water and barley in a large, heavy pot, and let soak for 1 hour.

2. Add the salt and bring to a boil. Cover, reduce the heat to low, and cook for 1 hour. Stir in the oil or Sour Dressing, and serve.

Per serving: Calories 144, Protein 4 g, Carbohydrates 32 g, Fat 0 g

Variations:
• Sauté a large sliced or chopped onion in the oil, and mix with the cooked barley.

• Add a sautéed onion (as above) along with 1 cup cooked white beans.

• Sauté a large sliced or chopped onion in the oil. Add ½ pound sliced or chopped mushrooms and sauté briefly, then mix with the cooked barley.

Hot Specialties

Mamaliga
(Corn Porridge)

Makes 6 servings

Corn came to Europe during the sixteenth century after the discovery of the Americas. It first arrived in Venice where it was used to make the porridge known as polenta, and eventually it was grown throughout Eastern Europe. Only in Romania and Georgia, however, did corn became a staple. In Romania, corn porridge was called "mamaliga," and peasants enjoyed it for breakfast, lunch, and dinner.

5 cups water
1⅓ cups yellow or white corn grits
1 teaspoon salt
¼ cup extra-virgin olive oil
1 cup Sour Dressing, p. 123 (optional)

1. Preheat the oven to 350°F. Oil a 3- or 4-quart casserole dish, and set aside.

2. Combine the water, corn grits, olive oil, and salt in a large, heavy bottomed saucepan, and bring to a boil. Reduce the heat to very low, cover, and cook, stirring occasionally, until all the water is absorbed and the thick paste comes away from the sides of the pan and is almost too thick to stir.

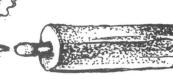

Hot Specialties

3. Spoon into the prepared casserole dish, and bake until lightly browned on top, about 20 minutes. Serve with Sour Dressing spooned over it, if desired.

Per serving: Calories 201, Protein 3 g, Carbohydrates 27 g, Fat 9 g

Tips:
• Do not be tempted to substitute cornmeal, as you will not have good results. Use only the more coarsely ground, whole-grain corn "grits" which can be found in natural food stores and some supermarkets.

• If the mixture sticks to the bottom of your saucepan, slip a flame tamer (also called a heat diffuser) underneath. For less stirring and sticking, after the grits come to a boil, transfer the mixture to a large double boiler to finish cooking.

Hot Specialties

Sweet Rice
with Prunes and Raisins

Makes 4 servings

Dried fruit adds a delicious sweet taste to this special dish.

3 tablespoons canola oil
1 large onion, coarsely chopped
1¼ cups long-grain brown rice, rinsed and drained
½ cup pitted prunes, cut in half or quartered
½ cup raisins
2 teaspoons ground cinnamon
Salt and pepper
3 cups water

1. Heat the oil in a large pot or Dutch oven. Add the onion and sauté until golden brown.

2. Add the rice and stir until it is well coated with oil. Add the raisins, prunes, cinnamon, salt, and pepper. Stir well, pour in the water, and bring to a boil. Reduce the heat to low, cover, and simmer until the rice is very tender and the water has been absorbed, about 1 hour.

3. Remove from the heat. Place a clean tea towel between the lid and the pot, and let rest for 10 minutes. (The towel will absorb any excess steam and moisture, helping to keep the rice from becoming mushy.)

Per serving: Calories 378, Protein 5 g, Carbohydrates 65 g, Fat 10 g

Hot Specialties

Millet

Makes 4 servings

Millet is one of the easiest grains to digest. Although it is most often served as a supper side dish, millet is also delicious as a breakfast porridge with a little fruit-sweetened jam, sugar, or maple syrup, and hot soymilk poured on top.

1 to 3 tablespoons canola oil
1 cup millet, rinsed and drained
2 cups boiling water
$\frac{1}{4}$ cup water
$\frac{1}{2}$ teaspoon salt

1. Put the oil in a heavy pan over medium-high heat. When hot, add the millet. Stir and fry for 3 to 5 minutes, or until the millet smells roasted and has turned a shade darker. Quickly and carefully pour in the 2 cups boiling water, cover, and set aside for 1 hour.

2. Uncover, add the $\frac{1}{4}$ cup water and salt, and bring to a boil again. Cover tightly, reduce the heat to very low, and cook gently for 40 minutes. Turn off the heat, cover, and let rest for at least 15 minutes.

Per serving: Calories 313, Protein 7 g, Carbohydrates 50 g, Fat 9 g

Variation:
• In a heavy pan or skillet, sauté 1 large sliced onion in 2 tablespoons of the oil until browned. Add to the millet along with the $\frac{1}{4}$ cup water and salt at the beginning of step 2. Proceed as directed.

Hot Specialties

Bulgur with Tomato Sauce

Makes 6 servings

Bulgur steeped in a sweet and spicy tomato sauce makes a delectable side dish.

3 cups tomato juice
1 cup water
5 tablespoons extra-virgin olive oil
1 teaspoon sugar
1 teaspoon salt
Pepper
2 cups bulgur

1. Combine the juice, water, oil, sugar, salt, and pepper in a large pot, and bring to a boil. Stir in the bulgur, then cover, reduce the heat, and simmer for 20 minutes.

2. Remove from the heat and let sit, covered, for 10 minutes or until the bulgur has absorbed the liquid and is plump and tender.

Per serving: Calories 276, Protein 6 g, Carbohydrates 37 g, Fat 10 g

Hot Specialties

Hungarian Cauliflower Paprikash

Makes 4 servings

Cauliflower makes a delicious substitute for the chicken that is traditionally used in this recipe. In Hungary and Czechoslovakia, paprikash was served with rice; in Romania and Transylvania, it was eaten with mamaliga, pp. 160-61.

3 tablespoons extra-virgin olive oil
1 large onion, chopped
1 red or green bell pepper, sliced
3 ripe tomatoes, peeled and chopped
1 tablespoon paprika
1 teaspoon sugar
Salt and cayenne pepper
1 medium cauliflower, cut into bite-size florets
Sour Dressing, p. 123 (optional)

1. Heat the oil in a large skillet. Add the onion and pepper, and sauté until soft.

2. Add the tomatoes, paprika, sugar, salt, and cayenne pepper, and mix well.

3. Add the cauliflower, cover, and simmer, stirring often, until tender (about 20 to 30 minutes). Add a little water if the mixture becomes too dry. If desired, spoon a dollop of Sour Dressing over each serving, or pass a bowl of Sour Dressing at the table.

Per serving: Calories 147, Protein 2 g, Carbohydrates 12 g, Fat 9 g

Hot Specialties

Tzimmes
(Fruit and Vegetable Casserole)

Makes 8 servings

Tzimmes is the general term for a sweet vegetable dish. The popular meaning of the Yiddish word — a mix-up or a big production — is based on the fact that tzimmes contains a variety of ingredients that are mixed and cooked together over a long period of time. Although it may sound like a long procedure, once it's in the oven the work is done. There is really no definitive recipe for tzimmes. The ingredients and flavorings that go into this classic dish vary according to locality and the individual cook.

6 large sweet potatoes or yams, peeled and cut into rounds or
    chunks
4 large carrots, cut in half lengthwise and sliced into chunks
1 cup pitted prunes
1 cup dried apricots
½ cup orange juice
⅓ cup sugar
½ teaspoon ground cinnamon
¼ teaspoon ground allspice
Good pinch of ground nutmeg
2 cups boiling water

1. Preheat the oven to 325°F. Oil a 9 x 13-inch baking dish, or mist it with nonstick cooking spray.

2. In a large bowl, combine the sweet potatoes, carrots, prunes, and apricots. In a small bowl, combine the orange juice, sugar, and spices. Pour over the vegetables and fruit, and mix gently. Spoon into the prepared baking dish.

3. Carefully pour the boiling water over the mixture. Cover tightly with a lid or silver foil, and bake for 1½ hours. Very carefully remove the lid or foil away from you so you don't get burned by the steam. Stir the tzimmes gently before serving. Serve hot.

Per serving: Calories 227, Protein 2 g, Carbohydrates 53 g, Fat 0 g

Variations:
• Use 3 sweet potatoes and 3 white potatoes.

• Add ½ teaspoon ground ginger.

• Replace the carrots with a small butternut squash, peeled and cut into bite-size chunks.

• Use chopped dried peaches instead of the apricots.

• Add the zest of 1 lemon and 1 orange.

• Reduce the orange juice to ⅓ cup and add 2 tablespoons fresh lemon juice.

• Omit the apricots and add 2 Granny Smith apples, peeled, cored, and sliced into thick wedges.

Hot Specialties

Sweet Carrots

Makes 6 servings

In Yiddish lore, sliced carrots are associated with gold coins. They are a symbol of prosperity and good fortune.

3 tablespoons canola oil
1½ pounds carrots, sliced
½ cup orange juice
2 tablespoons brown rice syrup, pure maple syrup, or sugar
¼ teaspoon ground ginger
Water, as needed

1. Heat the oil in a large pot or skillet. Add the carrots and stir until they are well coated.

2. Add the remaining ingredients, pouring in just enough water to barely cover. Bring to a boil. Reduce the heat, cover, and simmer gently for 20 minutes.

3. Remove the lid and continue cooking until the carrots are tender and the liquid has been reduced to a shiny glaze, about 10 minutes longer.

Per serving: Calories 135, Protein 1 g, Carbohydrates 17 g, Fat 7 g

Variation:
• Omit the orange juice and ginger. Season with 1 teaspoon ground cinnamon or a pinch of ground nutmeg. Add 2 tablespoons currants or raisins during the last 10 minutes of cooking.

Hot Specialties

Mujaddra
(Lentils and Rice)

Makes 4 to 6 servings

Variations of this stick-to-your-ribs staple from the Middle East are enjoyed the world over.

4 cups water
1 cup dried lentils, rinsed and drained
1 cup brown rice, rinsed and drained
2 large onions, julienned
¼ cup extra-virgin olive oil
1½ to 2 teaspoons salt

1. Combine the water, lentils, and rice in a large pot or Dutch oven, and bring to a boil. Reduce the heat to low, cover, and simmer until the lentils and rice are tender, about 1 hour and 15 minutes.

2. Meanwhile, sauté the onions in the oil over very low heat until very dark brown and caramelized, about 45 to 60 minutes. Stir into the cooked lentils and rice along with the salt to taste. Mix well. Serve hot.

Per serving: Calories 301, Protein 9 g, Carbohydrates 41 g, Fat 11 g

Hot Specialties

Mujaddra and Bulgur
(Lentils and Bulgur)

Makes 4 to 6 servings

Bulgur makes a hearty replacement for rice in this popular Middle Eastern mainstay.

4 cups water
1 cup dried lentils, rinsed and drained
1 cup bulgur
2 large onions, julienned
¼ cup extra-virgin olive oil
1½ to 2 teaspoons salt

1. Combine the water and lentils in a large pot or Dutch oven, and bring to a boil. Reduce the heat to low, cover, and simmer 45 minutes. Stir in the bulgur, cover, and simmer 30 minutes longer.

2. Meanwhile, sauté the onions in the oil over very low heat until very dark brown and caramelized, about 45 to 60 minutes. Stir into the cooked lentils and bulgur along with the salt to taste. Mix well. Serve hot.

Per serving: Calories 299, Protein 10 g, Carbohydrates 40 g, Fat 10 g

Variation:
• For **Mujaddra and Quinoa**, replace the bulgur with 1 cup quinoa, rinsed well and drained.

Hot Specialties

Lentils with Noodles

Makes 8 servings

A unique bean and noodle dish that warms both the body and spirit.

2 cups dried lentils, rinsed and drained
4 cups water
6 tablespoons extra-virgin olive oil
1 large onion, chopped
1 teaspoon crushed garlic
1 pound fettuccine
½ cup minced fresh parsley or cilantro
Salt and pepper
Lemon wedges (optional)

1. Combine the lentils and water in a large pot or Dutch oven, and bring to a boil. Reduce the heat, cover, and simmer until tender, about 30 minutes. Drain and return to the pot.

2. Heat 3 tablespoons of the olive oil in a large pot. Add the onion and sauté over very low heat until dark brown and caramelized, about 30 to 60 minutes. Stir in the garlic and remove from the heat.

3. Cook the pasta in boiling salted water until tender. Drain and combine with the lentils and onion. Add the remaining 3 tablespoons olive oil, parsley or cilantro, salt, and pepper. Stir well and heat through. Serve with lemon wedges, if desired.

Per serving: Calories 376, Protein 16 g, Carbohydrates 51 g, Fat 11 g

Hot Specialties

Unstuffed Holishkes
(Unrolled Cabbage Leaves)

Makes 4 servings

This time-saving version of Eastern European cabbage rolls has all the authentic original flavor without all the tedious fuss and work.

2 cups water
½ cup brown rice
2 tablespoons extra-virgin olive oil
1 cup chopped onions
1 cup sliced carrots
1 stalk celery, finely chopped
½ teaspoon crushed garlic
6 cups coarsely chopped green cabbage
1 cup tomato sauce
2 tablespoons sugar
1 tablespoon paprika
1 teaspoon dried oregano
½ teaspoon salt

1. Combine the water and rice in a large soup pot or Dutch oven, and bring to a boil. Reduce the heat to low, cover, and cook undisturbed for 1 hour.

2. About 20 minutes before the rice is ready, heat the oil in a large skillet. Add the onions, carrots, celery, and garlic, and sauté for 20 minutes. Add to the rice along with the remaining ingredients, and bring to a boil. Lower the heat, cover, and simmer for 30 minutes or until the cabbage is tender, stirring occasionally.

Per serving: Calories 205, Protein 3 g, Carbohydrates 32 g, Fat 7 g

Hot Specialties

Cabbage and Noodles

Makes 6 to 8 servings

Originating in the kitchens of German, Polish, and Hungarian peasantry, this simple combination of cabbage and noodles is filling and tasty. It makes good use of the homely green cabbage, a vegetable that survives early frost and stores well during cold winters.

¼ cup extra-virgin olive oil
2 large onions, julienned or chopped
1 large green cabbage
1 pound bow-tie noodles, cooked and drained
Salt and pepper

1. Heat the oil in a large pot or Dutch oven. Add the onion and sauté over low heat until golden brown, about 20 to 30 minutes.

2. Remove the outer leaves of the cabbage. Cut the cabbage into quarters through the stem end, then cut out the core. Slice into thin ribbons or finely chop. Add to the onions, cover, and cook over low heat, stirring often, until soft. If the vegetables stick to the bottom of the pan, add a small amount of water. Do not brown the cabbage.

3. Season with salt and plenty of pepper, then mix in the cooked noodles. Serve hot.

Per serving: Calories 169, Protein 3 g, Carbohydrates 21 g, Fat 8 g

Variation:
• Before adding the cabbage, sprinkle 1 teaspoon paprika over the onion and stir in 1 teaspoon caraway seeds, crushed slightly with the back of a spoon or ground.

Hot Specialties

Oct 5·2008 "10"

Red Cabbage and Apples

Makes 6 servings

This Polish and German favorite makes a delicious vegetable side dish or relish with any meal.

2 tart apples (such as Granny Smith), peeled and grated
2 tablespoons fresh lemon juice
4 cups shredded red cabbage (Cut out the core before
     shredding.)
½ cup water
¼ cup cider or wine vinegar
2 tablespoons olive or canola oil
1½ tablespoons sugar
Salt and pepper

1. Grate the apples and mix with the lemon juice.

2. Put the apples and cabbage in a large pan with a tight-fitting lid. Stir in the remaining ingredients, and season with salt and pepper. Mix well and bring to a boil. Reduce the heat to low, and steam for 20 minutes or until the cabbage is very soft. Serve hot or cold.

Per serving: Calories 95, Protein 0 g, Carbohydrates 13 g, Fat 5 g

Variations:
• Replace the vinegar with an additional ¼ cup fresh lemon juice.

• Sauté a chopped onion in the oil to begin with. Then add the remaining ingredients and proceed as directed.

• Add about ¼ cup raisins to the main recipe or any of the above variations.

Hot Specialties

White Cabbage
with Sour Dressing

Makes 6 servings

This traditional treatment of cabbage imparts an elegant touch.

1 small white cabbage
¼ cup water
3 tablespoons olive or canola oil
Salt and pepper
1 cup Sour Dressing, p. 123

1. Remove the outer leaves of the cabbage. Cut the cabbage into quarters through the stem end, then cut out the core. Slice into thin ribbons and put in a large pan with a tight-fitting lid. Add the water, oil, and a pinch of salt and pepper. Bring up to a simmer, cover, and cook until the cabbage is very soft, about 20 minutes. Do not add any additional water during cooking.

2. Remove from the heat and stir in the Sour Dressing. Warm over low heat for 5 to 8 minutes, just until heated through. Do not boil.

Per serving: Calories 125, Protein 4 g, Carbohydrates 3 g, Fat 11 g

Variations:
• Add 2 teaspoons of caraway seeds at the start.

• For a sweet and sour flavor, add a tablespoon or two of fresh lemon juice or vinegar and an equal amount of sugar.

Hot Specialties

Fruit Dishes

Hot Apples

Makes 4 to 6 servings

Tender, sweet apples make a unique and delicious side dish.

1 pound apples (about 3 medium)
2 tablespoons fresh lemon juice
1 tablespoon water
1 to 2 tablespoons sugar
½ teaspoon ground cinnamon

1. Peel, core, and slice the apples. Place in a large skillet with the lemon juice and water. Cover and steam over low heat until the apples are very tender and starting to fall apart, about 10 minutes.

2. Add the sugar and cinnamon, and mash slightly with a potato masher or fork. Serve hot.

Per serving: Calories 64, Protein 0 g, Carbohydrates 15 g, Fat 0 g

Variation:
• For **Hot and Creamy Apples**, omit the lemon juice and water and sauté the apples in 3 tablespoons canola oil until tender. Sprinkle with 1 to 2 tablespoons of sugar and 1 teaspoon of ground cinnamon. Stir in Sour Dressing, p. 123, to taste.

Fruit Dishes

Applesauce

Makes about 4 cups

Spring, summer, and fall are great times to make homemade applesauce. If you prepare a large quantity, freeze some so you can have fresh homemade flavor even in the winter. Homemade applesauce will keep in the freezer for about six months. Try combining a few different varieties of apples for the best taste.

8 to 10 large apples (Jonathan, Rome Beauty, Cortland,
    Northern Spy, York Imperial, etc.)
About 1/2 cup water, as needed
1/2 teaspoon vanilla extract (optional)
1/2 teaspoon ground cinnamon (optional)

Food Mill Method:
The food mill method uses the whole apple — skin, seeds, and core — so nutrition is maximized and preparation time is minimal. Try to find organic apples, especially since these will not be peeled. You'll need a food mill to separate the pulp from the rest of the apple. Food mills are available in cookware stores. (Foley is a popular brand.) If you like applesauce, it's definitely worth the investment. There's no better way to make it from the standpoints of convenience, flavor, and nutrition.

1. Wash the apples and cut them into quarters. Do not peel or core. Pour just enough water into a large pot or Dutch oven so that the bottom of the pan is covered. Add the apples, cover, and cook over medium heat until the apples are very soft and starting to fall apart.

2. Place a food mill over a large bowl. Remove the apples with a slotted spoon, and place them in batches in the food mill. Process the apples through the mill; the applesauce will drop into the bowl below and the peels, seeds, and core will remain in the mill. Clean out the food mill as often as necessary during processing.

Fruit Dishes

3. Stir the vanilla extract and cinnamon into the applesauce, if desired. Serve warm or chilled.

Peel & Core Method:
This method calls for peeling and coring the apples before cooking. There's more preparation beforehand than for the food mill method, but less clean-up afterwards.

1. Wash the apples. Peel, core, and cut them into quarters.

2. Pour just enough water into a large pot or Dutch oven so that the bottom of the pan is covered. Add the apples, cover, and cook over medium heat until the apples are very soft and starting to fall apart.

3. Mash with a potato masher or fork, or leave as is if you like a chunky applesauce. Stir in the vanilla extract and cinnamon, if desired. Serve warm or chilled.

Per cup: Calories 182, Protein 1 g, Carbohydrates 43 g, Fat 0 g

Tips:
• If your apples are very tart or if you prefer a sweeter apple-sauce, use apple juice or apple juice concentrate instead of water.

• Some apples are drier or juicier than others, so you may need to add a little more liquid during cooking if the apples stick to the bottom of the pan. The less liquid you use the thicker the sauce will be.

Stewed Prunes

Makes about 1½ cups (about 3 to 4 servings)

A naturally sweet treat for young and old alike. Rich in minerals, fiber, and flavor.

1 cup whole pitted prunes
1 cup water

Combine the prunes and water in a small saucepan, and bring to a boil. Reduce the heat, cover, and simmer until the prunes are tender, about 20 minutes. Serve warm or chilled.

Per serving: Calories 100, Protein 1 g, Carbohydrates 26 g, Fat 0 g

Fruit Dishes

Dried Fruit Compote

Makes 4½ cups

Stewed fruit is a wonderful treat for breakfast, snacks, or dessert. It keeps for several weeks in the refrigerator.

Fruit Mix:
4 cups water
2 cups chopped mixed dried fruit (such as prunes, peaches, apples, apricots, raisins, dates, pears, figs, etc.)

Flavoring Options:
1 stick of cinnamon, broken into 3 pieces
2 thin slices of lemon
2 thin slices of orange
1 teaspoon vanilla extract

1. Combine the fruit mix and any flavoring options of your choice in a large saucepan, and bring to a boil.

2. Remove from the heat, cover, and let rest until cooled to room temperature. Transfer to a storage container, and chill in the refrigerator.

Per ½ cup: Calories 97, Protein 1 g, Carbohydrates 23 g, Fat 0 g

Fruit Dishes

Fresh Fruit Compote

Makes 2 to 4 servings

A simmered fruit mixture with a tender texture and no added sweeteners. Great as an appetizer, dessert, side dish, breakfast dish, or wholesome snack.

1 Granny Smith apple, peeled and chunked
1 pear, peeled and chunked
1 cup water
¼ cup chopped dates, figs, or raisins
½ teaspoon ground cinnamon

Combine all the ingredients in a saucepan, and bring to a boil. Simmer, stirring occasionally, until the fruit is tender but not mushy. Serve hot, warm, or chilled.

Per serving: Calories 100, Protein 1 g, Carbohydrates 24 g, Fat 0 g

Tip:
• If the compote gets too sweet, add 2 to 3 teaspoons fresh lemon juice to balance the flavor.

Freestyle Fruit Salad

Apple, chunked
Grapefruit, peeled, sectioned, seeded, and pith removed
Orange, peeled, sectioned, seeded, and pith removed
Banana, sliced
Melon chunks or balls
Blueberries
Orange juice

Combine the fruits of your choice in a large, nonmetallic bowl. Add orange juice to cover. Serve at once or cover and chill.

Fruit Dishes

Ambrosia

Makes 2 servings

Food of the gods!

1 navel orange, peeled, sectioned, and cut into bite-size pieces
1 crisp apple, cut into bite-size chunks (optional)
1 ripe banana, cut in half lengthwise and sliced
¼ cup coarsely chopped walnuts
¼ cup raisins
2 tablespoons shredded dried coconut
¼ cup fresh lemon juice
Sweetener of your choice
Ground cinnamon, cardamom, allspice, or nutmeg (optional)

1. In a medium nonmetallic bowl, toss together the fruit, nuts, raisins, and coconut.

2. In a separate small bowl, whisk together the lemon juice and sweetener to taste. Pour over the fruit and toss gently.

3. Just before serving, dust the top of the salad very lightly with cinnamon, cardamom, allspice, or nutmeg, or a mixture made with a pinch of all four spices, if desired.

Per serving: Calories 377, Protein 4 g, Carbohydrates 49 g, Fat 17 g

Fruit Dishes

Cranberry Relish

Makes 2 cups

This crunchy "raw" relish is best made in a food processor, because cranberries are difficult to chop by hand.

2 cups cranberries, rinsed and drained
1 navel orange, peeled, sectioned, and cut into chunks
¾ cup pecans or walnuts
½ cup pure maple syrup or brown rice syrup

Place the cranberries, orange sections, and nuts in a food processor, and pulse until finely minced. Stir in the syrup. Chill several hours before serving.

Per 2 tablespoons: Calories 70, Protein 0 g, Carbohydrates 10 g, Fat 3 g

Tip:
• Oranges other than navels may be used, if preferred. Just be sure to thoroughly remove the pith and seeds.

Fruit Dishes

Orange, Radish, and Black Olive Salad

Makes 6 to 8 servings

A popular Moroccan salad with a distinctively different taste.

4 oranges, peeled and pith removed
½ cup sliced radishes (optional)
2 to 3 tablespoons fresh lemon juice or wine vinegar
2 tablespoons extra-virgin olive oil
½ teaspoon crushed garlic
Salt
8 to 12 black olives
1 teaspoon cumin (optional)
1 teaspoon paprika
Pinch of cayenne pepper

1. Slice the oranges, then cut into bite-size pieces. Place in a bowl with the radishes, if using.

2. Dress with the lemon juice or vinegar, oil, garlic, and salt, and toss gently. Add the olives and toss again. Serve sprinkled with cumin, if using, paprika, and cayenne.

Per serving: Calories 80, Protein 1 g, Carbohydrates 9 g, Fat 4 g

Fruit Dishes

Index

Index

Index

Also by Joanne Stepaniak

The Saucy Vegetarian $12.95

The Uncheese Cookbook $12.95

Vegan Vittles $12.95

Delicious Food for a Healthy Heart $12.95

Ecological Cooking $12.95 (with Kathy Hecker)

The Nutritional Yeast Cookbook $9.95

Table for Two $12.95

Purchase these vegetarian cookbooks from your local bookstore or natural foods store, or you can buy them directly from:
Book Publishing Company
P.O. Box 99
Summertown, TN 38483
1-800-695-2241

Please include $3.50 per book for shipping and handling.

To find your favorite vegetarian and soyfood products online, visit:
www.healthy-eating.com